Making the Bible Yours

Making the Bible Yours

by
Earl C. Wolf

Beacon Hill Press of Kansas City
Kansas City, Missouri

Thirteenth Printing, 1984

This book is a revision of
The Living Word, by the same author.

ISBN: 0-8341-0892-5

Printed in the United States of America

Cover art: Crandall Vail

Acknowledgments

I wish to express my gratitude to the American Bible Society for the most helpful materials, which they furnished. Thanks is due the Fleming H. Revell Company for the permission to use the poem "The Anvil of God's Word," by John Clifford, in *The Best Loved Religious Poems,* by James Gilchrist Lawson. Thanks is due also the Moody Press of Chicago for permission to use the poem "The Bible! There It Stands!" in *How to Master the English Bible,* by James M. Gray. Publishers have been most courteous. Other permissions have been acknowledged in the Notes.

To
Mildred

and our three:

Timothy Earl
Stephen Nicholas
and Earlene Elizabeth

THE BIBLE!
THERE IT STANDS!

Where childhood needs a standard
  Or youth a beacon light,
Where sorrow sighs for comfort
  Or weakness longs for might,
Bring forth the Holy Bible,
  The Bible! There it stands!
Resolving all life's problems
  And meeting its demands.

Though sophistry conceal it,
  The Bible! There it stands!
Though Pharisees profane it,
  Its influence expands;
It fills the world with fragrance
  Whose sweetness never cloys;
It lifts our eyes to heaven;
  It heightens human joys.

Despised and torn in pieces,
  By infidels decried—
The thunderbolts of hatred
  The haughty cynics' pride—
All these have railed against it
  In this and other lands,
Yet dynasties have fallen,
  And still the Bible stands!

To paradise a highway,
    The Bible! There it stands!
Its promises unfailing,
    Nor grievous its commands;
It points man to the Saviour,
    The Lover of his soul;
Salvation is its watchword,
    Eternity its goal!

                        —ANONYMOUS

Contents

Preface	10
Introduction	12
Part I—Teach Me Thy Statutes	
A Bible Reading and Study Guide	
1. Make the Bible Yours	19
2. Practical Guides for Bible Reading	28
3. Simple Methods for Bible Study	40
Part II—Thy Word in My Heart	
A Scripture Memorization Manual	
4. Memorizing the Scriptures	63
5. A Scripture Memorization Plan	77
6. Additional Suggestions for Memorization	87
Notes	100
Bibliography	102

Preface

When the late Dr. Lauriston J. DuBois was executive secretary of the Nazarene Young People's Society (1948-56), he invited me to write this book to give guidance in the reading and studying of God's Word and to give encouragement and concrete suggestions to help especially young persons and new Christians to develop the habit of memorizing the Scriptures. I was delighted to take on the assignment, which came to fruition partly through the valuable assistance of Mrs. Edwin K. Bean, of Norristown, Pa., in preparing the manuscript.

It is my firm conviction that many Christians live in the shallows of life when they could be enjoying the deep things of the Spirit. The spiritual life is strengthened when we spend time with the Word and let God speak to us. Aspirations and attainments are inseparable. Not accidentally, but intentionally do we come "unto the measure of the stature of the fulness of Christ" (Eph. 4:13). Bible reading and study are indispensable to Christian maturity.

Part I, "Teach Me Thy Statutes," has been designed to help you find some workable plan and organization for your own Bible reading and study. A lifetime of study cannot exhaust the treasures of the Scriptures. I trust that you will gain also a new sense of urgency in making the Bible a part of your daily life. Although there are many values to be gained from reading and studying God's Word, I know that you will find above all else a source of strength for your own spiritual life and a Book that answers your *heart* needs. I hope it will lead you to pray as did the Psalmist, "Teach me Thy statutes."

Part II, "Thy Word in My Heart," gives practical suggestions and a workable plan for your own Bible memorization. Within the heart of every true Christian flames the desire to make the most of one's spiritual life. It is imperative, then, that attention be given to reading, studying, and memorizing the Word of God.

Many earnest and sincere young people and new Christians fail to hide the Word of God away in their hearts because of the lack of practical suggestions. The question that confronts them is: "Where and how shall I begin?" It is the task of the church to give them a workable plan and sufficient guidance to mark out the way ahead in this important endeavor. It is hoped that this manual will prove to be a blessing along this line and will fill a pressing need.

"Thy word have I hid in mine heart, that I might not sin against thee" (Ps. 119:11). The weapon that wins in the hour of temptation is the Word previously stored in the memory. It was the Master's instrument of victory in the wilderness. David and Christ provide sufficient *recommendation* for memorizing the Word. The values of scripture memorization are many. Pray that a new sense of urgency might come upon you and that God will help you as you *begin today* to hide His Word away in your heart.

I am indebted to Milton Poole for the Scripture Memorization Plan found in Part II, Chapter 2, and I'm grateful to Mrs. G. B. Williamson, who has so effectively used the Bible for oral readings, for the "Selections for Oral Bible Readings" as found in Chapter 3. In this book as in all my endeavors for the Kingdom down through the years, my wife was a constant encouragement and offered goodly criticisms and suggestions. Others have been kind and helpful and to them I want to express my sincere thanks.

It is my prayer and hope that this manual will be a practical means of helping you to fill your mind and heart with the treasures of the eternal Word.

—EARL C. WOLF

Introduction

It is not difficult for us to agree to the proposition that the Bible is the Book of the Christian religion. Many of us will give assent to the proposition that the individual Christian ought to know the Bible. All too few of us, however, are busy at the task of making the Bible our own.

Perhaps you as a reader are a new Christian. Perhaps you have only recently found Christ as your Savior. Perhaps you have walked with Christ for many years. No matter; may I take this opportunity to urge you to attach yourself to the Word of God, your Bible, and never get away from it.

It has been our intention that this book by Earl C. Wolf will be a practical handbook that will give you the simple ABCs of Bible study and Bible reading that you want. We hope and pray that it will be to you, the reader, the practical help for which you have been looking and even praying.

First of all, get a Bible—one of your own, your very own. Perhaps you will want a copy of the New Testament also. Your Bible does not have to be expensive. There are Bibles available very inexpensively, so that no person need say he cannot afford one. Or if you feel you cannot possibly afford to buy a Bible, contact your pastor and without doubt he will find a way that you can obtain one.

Second, carry your Bible. Every Christian should be a Bible-carrying Christian. A Bible under the arm is a testimony to the world around as to what we believe. Let us begin early in our Christian lives to develop the habit of carrying the Word of God as we go to the house of God. It is also a good habit to have a small, pocket-sized New Testament which we can carry at all times: to work, to school, and everywhere we go.

Third, read the Bible, study the Bible, memorize portions of the Bible. It is the purpose of this little book you have in your hand to help you in these tasks.

Dr. Robert Taylor, one-time secretary of the American Bible Society, told us repeatedly that their surveys show that Bible-reading Christians are those who early in their lives built a habit of Bible reading. He also said that they had yet to find a person who really built that habit who ever got away from it. This should be an encouragement to us and also a warning. We have this very important phase of our Christian lives before us and we would not fail in it. Let us not miss the glorious privileges which lie ahead of us as we live with our Bibles.

The author is himself a student of the Word and a lover of the Word. Much of what he has given us has come out of his own experience as a Christian and as a leader of youth.

—Lauriston J. DuBois

Part I

TEACH ME THY STATUTES

A Bible Reading and Study Guide

THE BIBLE

When I am tired, the Bible is my bed;
   Or in the dark, the Bible is my light.
When I am hungry, it is vital bread;
   Or fearful, it is armor for the fight.
When I am sick, 'tis healing medicine;
Or lonely, thronging friends I find therein.

If I would work, the Bible is my tool;
   Or play, it is a harp of happy sound.
If I am ignorant, it is my school;
   If I am sinking, it is solid ground;
If I am cold, the Bible is my fire;
And it is wings if boldly I aspire.

Should I be lost, the Bible is my guide;
   Or naked, it is raiment rich and warm.
Am I imprisoned, it is ranges wide;
   Or tempest-tossed, a shelter from the storm,
Would I adventure, 'tis a gallant sea;
Or would I rest, it is a flowery lea.

Does gloom oppress? The Bible is my sun.
   Or ugliness? It is a garden fair.
Am I athirst? How cool its currents run!
   Or stifled? What a vivifying air!
Since thus thou gavest thyself to me,
How shall I give myself, great Book, to thee?

—AMOS R. WELLS

The Bible

"This Book contains—the mind of God, the state of man, the way of salvation, doom of sinners, and happiness of believers. Its doctrines are holy, its precepts are binding, its histories are true, and its decisions are immutable. Read it to be wise, believe it to be safe, and practice it to be holy. It contains light to direct you, food to support you, and comfort to cheer you. It is the traveller's map, the pilgrim's staff, the pilot's compass, the soldier's sword, and the Christian's charter. Here Paradise is restored, Heaven is opened, and the gate of Hell disclosed. CHRIST is Its Grand Subject, our good is its design, and the glory of God its end. It should fill the memory, rule the heart, and guide the feet. Read it slowly, frequently, prayerfully. It is a mine of wealth, a paradise of glory, and a river of pleasure. It is given you in life, will be open at the judgment, and be remembered forever. It involves the highest responsibility, rewards the greatest labor, and condemns all who trifle with its holy contents."

—*Selected*

"Scripture contains pools at which lambs can drink, and depths in which elephants must swim" (Augustine).

When I Read My Bible Through

I supposed I knew my Bible,
   Reading piecemeal, hit or miss,
Now a bit of John or Matthew,
   Now a snatch of Genesis;
Certain chapters of Isaiah,
   Certain psalms (the twenty-third),
Twelfth of Romans, first of Proverbs—
   Yes, I thought I knew the Word,
But I found a thorough reading
   Was a different thing to do.
And the way was unfamiliar
   When I read my Bible through.

You who like to play at Bible,
   Dip and dabble here and there,
Just before you kneel a-weary
   And yawn out a hurried prayer;
You who treat the "Crown of Writings"
   As you treat no other book—
Just a paragraph, disjointed,
   Just a crude, impatient look—
Try a worthier procedure,
   Try a broad, a steady view—
You will kneel in very rapture
   When you read your Bible through!

—Amos R. Wells

1

Make the Bible Yours

At the age of 11, John Wanamaker, the merchant prince, purchased a Bible. In later years he said regarding this purchase: "I have of course made large purchases of property in my time, involving millions of dollars. But it was as a boy in the country, at the age of 11 years, that I made my greatest purchase. In the little mission Sunday School I bought a small red leather Bible for $2.75, which I paid for in small installments. Looking back over my life, I see that that little red Book was the foundation on which my life has been built and has made possible all that has counted in my life. I know now that it was the greatest investment and the most important and far-reaching purchase I ever made."[1]

"Man shall not live by bread alone, but by every word that proceedeth out of the mouth of God" (Matt. 4:4). Thus Jesus answered Satan in His first temptation in the wilderness. "It is written," said Jesus and the victory was won by the use of the unchangeable, eternal Word; for it was the Sword of the Spirit that foiled the tempter and gave Christ the victory. In this Book we have the weapons of our warfare. When we need strength to conquer, we must have the sustenance of God's Word. We simply cannot afford to live without a knowledge of the Bible. Said Woodrow Wilson, "A man has deprived himself of the best there is in the world who has deprived himself of this, a knowledge of the Bible."

The Bible is life's supreme Guidebook. The Psalmist

prayed, "Teach me thy statutes." It is not enough for us to read religious books and periodicals, to hear sermons and addresses, or to attend the services of the church, as excellent as all these may be. We must know the Word of God for ourselves. We need the resources of this Guidebook and we ought to have those treasures that lie hidden from the casual or careless reader. We may enjoy their story, astronomy, science, psychology, geology, philosophy, poetry, biology, ethics, prophecy, and the literature of the Bible. We need, however, to look upon the Word as God's unique revelation of His will and seek to open our hearts for the guidance of God in our lives.

The Book for Believers

Even the man who professes no faith will read the Word of God with profit. The Bible, however, is fundamentally a religious Book, and its eternal verities are discovered by simple faith and not by reasoning nor by merely intellectual insight. The Holy Spirit, who inspired the writing of the Scriptures, is also the Word's best Interpreter. Dr. George F. Pentecost lists seven things that the Bible contains for believers. They are as follows:

1. The Bible, the only Book that can make us wise unto salvation.

2. The Word of God, the only authority in matters of faith and practice binding upon the conscience.

3. The Bible contains in itself the absolute guarantee of our inheritance in Christ.

4. The Word of God is the means appointed for the culture of our Christian life.

5. The Bible is the Christian's armory.

6. The Bible is a perfect map and chart to the Christian on pilgrimage through the world.

7. The Bible reveals things to come.[2]

The Bible ministers to life's deepest and greatest needs, for it is the Book of Life. Its promises have lifted many in their hours of perplexity or grief, and its words have brought victory in the time of temptation. David Livingstone said, "The future is as bright as the promises of God." The Bible gives daily strength for the journey and is indispensable for the hours of life's emergencies. The Word is essential to growth in grace and to spiritual development and is a practical Guide for living. It is a timely and timeless Book that hurdles the boundaries of territories and tongues and speaks to all men everywhere.

"At Thy Word I Will"

The Bible, if it truly be your Guidebook, must be more than read, studied, and memorized by you. It must be obeyed. The practical advice of James is, "But be ye doers of the word, and not hearers only, deceiving your own selves" (Jas. 1:22).

The importance of obedience is graphically illustrated by the story of the four fishermen of Galilee, as recorded in Luke 5:1-11. Notice the pivotal point that obedience plays here.

> *Failure:* "We have toiled all the night, and have taken nothing."
>
> *Faith:* "Nevertheless at thy word."
>
> *Fortune:* "A great multitude of fishes."

The Word will truly be Bread for us and bring strength to our lives when we say, "At thy word I will."

The Bible for Your Needs

The illnesses of our modern society are evidences that we have spent fewer than the needed hours with the Word of God and in seeking to know God's will for our lives. Dr. A. T.

Pierson classifies under seven divisions the 12 conspicuous symbols "chosen in the Word of God to represent its uses and the range and scope of its application to all human need."

1. The *mirror,* to show us ourselves as we are and may be (Jas. 1:25).

2. The *laver,* to wash away our sins and our defilement (Eph. 5:26).

3. The *lamp and light,* to guide us in the right way (Ps. 119:105).

4. The *milk, bread, strong meat, and honey,* affording sustenance and satisfaction to the believer at all stages of spiritual development (Heb. 5:12-14; Ps. 19:10).

5. The fine *gold,* to enrich us with heavenly treasure (Ps. 19:10).

6. The *fire, hammer, sword,* to be used in the warfare of life (Jer. 23:29; Heb. 4:12; Eph. 6:17).

7. The *seed,* to beget souls in God's image, and to plant harvest fields for God (Jas. 1:18; 1 Pet. 1:23; Matthew 13).[3]

The Seven Wonders of the Bible

A number of years ago I heard Rev. John A. Huffman, then assistant pastor of the Park Street Congregational Church of Boston, preaching on the Bible and he gave the following list of the wonders of the Word:

1. The wonder of its preservation and formation.

2. The wonder of its universal appeal.

3. The wonder of its great unification.

4. The wonder of its trustworthiness.

5. The wonder of its careful and frank presentation of facts.

6. The wonder of its central Personality—Christ.

7. The wonder of its victory and triumph over its many enemies.

"It was a wise colporteur who exhibited this poster in his book-stall, and his flair for touching the right note brought him many customers:

> **THE POWER OF A BOOK**
>
> If you love—
> Poetry, History, pure Morality,
> profound Thoughts,
> If you wish to become good
> and to be happy,
>
> **READ THE BIBLE,**
>
> The most inexpensive
> The most widespread   } of all books
> The most widely translated

A strange work is this Bible! One volume containing 66 different books which were written over a space of 1,600 years by more than 40 different authors: kings, poets, soldiers, philosophers, fishermen, shepherds, statesmen, and tax collectors. Scarcely any of the authors had any communication with the other, yet this volume shows marvelous unity. What other work has ever been compiled in like manner? Select the 66 best books on medical subjects written during the last 1,500 years by the 40 best authorities, allopaths, homoeopaths, hydropaths, etc. Collect them in one volume and see what you make of treating a sick man by their directions! The best medical and scientific books are out-of-date in 20 years.

"The Bible alone is never out-of-date. This Book maintains the level of progress through the ages. It even outstrips progress and becomes the leader of civilization. Unbelievers have hurled themselves against this Book, but have failed to take one page from its contents. World-powers have conspired to destroy it, and the Bible has been refuted, ridiculed, publicly burned, and has been condemned more than any other writing, but it is like the anvil which wears out every hammer.

"All the systems, all the philosophies, every manner of attack, every kind of violence have hurled themselves on this Book, yet without shaking it: they have been swept away and destroyed; the Book stands and will stand."[4]

THEME OF THE LONGEST CHAPTER

The 119th psalm is a little Bible in itself. Its single theme, treated in varied ways in its lines, is the Word of God. The various aspects of the will of God and the duties of the Christian are suggested by the 10 titles given for the Word of God. Those titles are:

1. The Way (v. 1)
2. The Law (v. 1)
3. The Testimonies (v. 2)
4. The Precepts (v. 4)
5. The Statutes (v. 5)
6. The Commandments (v. 6)
7. The Judgments (v. 7)
8. The Word (v. 9)
9. The Truth (v. 30)
10. The Righteousness (v. 40)

VOICES AT VARIANCE

Notice the voices at variance in our civilization today. There are those who are feverishly grasping for things. They have been crying, "Man shall live by bread alone." They have been caught in the currents of a culture that is far from being as vitally religious as it should be. The kind but insistent voice of the Master, however, reminds us that "man shall not live by bread alone." The prophet of centuries past says, "Wherefore do ye spend money for that which is not bread? and your labour for that which satisfieth not?" In a time when worlds are in collision, in a day of conflicting ideologies, in an hour when foundations seem to be crumbling, we most surely need to let God speak to us and saturate our souls with the word that shall help us toward a strong faith, a sturdy character, and a spiritual freedom upon which all other liberties are ultimately dependent.

MAKE THE BIBLE YOURS

The Bible has made a rich contribution to the literature of the world. It was the Source Book for that immortal allegory, *The Pilgrim's Progress,* written by John Bunyan in Bedford jail. William Shakespeare in his 37 plays alluded to 54 of the 66 books of the Bible. Milton, Chaucer, Browning, Dante, Kipling, and others drank of the water of this Well. The Bible has influenced the history of mankind and interprets ancient history for us. The Bible is the Source Book of Christian theology and here the doctrinal expressions of our faith have their foundation. Although the Bible has made its contribution to literature, history, and theology, its greatest blessing is its guidance for you in daily living.

You *must* make the Bible yours. You'll like its stories, enjoy its poetry, profit by its prayers, get a lift from its promises, live again with its biographies, be thrilled with its great chapters, receive in its pages light on the problems of life, find in its books freedom from fear, gain truth from its literature, and be nobly enriched by your acquaintance with the world's greatest Book of all.

The Time Is Now

Too many professed Christians and church members have neglected God's Word, perhaps because they have no adequate pattern for their Bible reading. The time to begin to give the Bible its rightful place in your life is NOW. In your youth and in the early day of a new Christian's life, you should plan to do something definite about making the Bible yours, for deep within every true Christian flames the desire to do something constructive and worthwhile about one's spiritual life. If you are to grow in grace, make your life count, and be a medium of blessing to others, you cannot delay in making your delight the Word of God. There is no telling how significant and far-reaching the habit of Bible reading and study will be to you in its ever-growing influence over the remaining years of your life. Do something about your plans NOW.

My Earnest Prayer

I trust that you will pray with the Psalmist today, "Teach me thy statutes." Do something definitely to make the Bible yours. Give yourself to the great Book that has been given to you. This is my earnest prayer for you.

The Anvil of God's Word

Last eve I paused beside the blacksmith's door,
  And heard the anvil ring the vesper chime;
Then looking in, I saw upon the floor
  Old hammers worn with beating years of time.

"How many anvils have you had," said I,
  "To wear and batter all these hammers so?"
"Just one," said he, and then with twinkling eye,
  "The anvil wears the hammers out, you know."

And so, I thought, the Anvil of God's Word
  For ages skeptic blows have beat upon;
Yet, though the noise of falling blows was heard,
  The Anvil is unharmed, the hammers gone.

JOHN CLIFFORD, D.D.

2

Practical Guides for Bible Reading

You must discover for your own use an adequate plan for Bible reading. That which is profitable to one person may not be so to another; therefore find that plan most suitable for your own purposes. Whatever you do, *find some plan and start today* to make the Bible *yours*. Your entire Christian life is dependent to a great measure for its success on what use you make of life's supreme Guidebook. The purpose of this chapter is to give you some guidance in making your Bible reading fruitful and enjoyable.

There are two fundamental considerations in this chapter. (1) There are some starting points and suggestions on the approach to effective Bible reading. The problem that presents itself is, "How shall I read my Bible?" (2) There are practical suggestions as to where I should begin with my reading. The question here is, "What shall I read?"

How Shall I Read My Bible?

1. *I must have a Bible of my own.* This is a preliminary consideration but an important one. Choose a Bible of your particular liking with the size and print that you desire. Bibles are available in many styles and in all price ranges. Many times you will want to pick up your pencil or pen, if the type of paper permits, and underline a certain word or phrase or

perhaps make some note in the margin. This practice is of value, but you can do it only with your own Bible. In underlining a word or phrase with your pen, you may permanently fix its treasures in your mind and heart. If perchance you cannot recall something that has been of blessing to you, the markings may help you to locate it. A verse that has brought a particular ministry to you in an hour of need deserves to be remembered. Make your markings meaningful and do not mark your Bible because others do or just for the sake of marking. May those markings indicate riches discovered.

2. *I must remember my daily appointment.* This engagement will take some of the tension out of our busy days. If we say that we are too busy to read God's Word daily, we are admitting that we consider other matters of more importance. Our values need a new arrangement. Many Christians *read* the newspaper and only *glance* at the Bible. It is of definite value for you to read the Bible regularly, and the failure to do so will eventually mean spiritual impoverishment. Regularity in the matter of the hours of eating, sleeping, and exercising has much to do with our physical well-being, for the human system responds to regularity. Likewise, regularity in our attention to the Word of God puts health and strength into our spiritual life and gives us resources that cannot be gained by spasmodic reading. The prophet Jeremiah suggests that daily reading is a normal procedure for the Christian when he talks about "eating" the Word. "Thy words were found, and I did eat them; and thy word was unto me the joy and rejoicing of mine heart: for I am called by thy name, O Lord God of hosts" (Jer. 15:16). An appetite for the Word is normal, and by daily use of the Book we receive our spiritual nourishment just as by the regular eating of food we obtain and maintain our physical strength.

Men and women in the armed forces, students in college and university dormitories, and members of large families may find it difficult to locate a quiet spot in the day's schedule. It will take determination to keep your appointment, but your discipline will have its reward. Do not parade your Christian practices nor be ashamed of them.

3. *I must set a definite time.* In as far as possible, our appointment with the Word should be at the same time each day. This practice is not always feasible where working hours change from week to week and where schedules are often interrupted. A definite time, however, should be kept when it is reasonably possible. Even though the time may vary, find a few moments each day for life's needs.

The preferable and most profitable time for Bible reading for many people is in the morning, when they are mentally and physically rested and are able to bring their best to God's Book. A godly layman, whom it was my privilege to pastor for nearly six years, made it a practice to spend time in Bible reading and prayer in the early hours of the morning before going to a day of hard labor in the steel mill. His testimonies were filled with the Scriptures. We cannot afford to step out into the storm and stress of the day without adequate resources. New light gained in meditation may provide a needed challenge that day.

4. *I must come to the Bible prayerfully.* You will never see the shadow on the dial without the shining of the sun. Essential, likewise, is the help of the Holy Spirit in the interpretation of God's Word to us. John wrote in his Gospel, "Howbeit when he, the Spirit of truth, is come, he will guide you into all truth" (John 16:13; see also 1 Cor. 2:11-12). The Holy Spirit is our Interpreter, our Teacher, and our Guide. The Psalmist prayed, "Open thou mine eyes, that I may behold wondrous things out of thy law" (Ps. 119:18). I must ask and trust God to speak out of His treasure to my heart.

5. *I must read effectively, not mechanically.* It is better to read and understand two verses than to run slipshod through

two chapters. Read for light on your problems, for food for your soul, for strength for your day, for rest from the tensions, and for guidance toward victorious living. Some may read a chapter or two and others only a few verses or a paragraph with profit each day. Make your reading effective and do not read merely to count pages or chapters. Do not permit your reading to drift into the routine of mathematical accomplishments, but keep it fresh and seek to let God's voice speak to you each day from those sacred pages. Then will your mind be enlightened, your motions nourished, and your will strengthened.

6. *I must read purposefully.* I should read God's Word with anticipation. I should meditate upon the Scriptures and expect God to speak to me and let me know His message for me today. Only this expectant attitude can make the Word a practical Guide for my everyday living. The Bible is a Mirror in which you may discover for yourself the weaknesses, failures, and needs of your life. Walk in the light of its truth and new advances in spiritual development will be yours. You have not spent a sufficient amount of time with the Word unless you go from its pages with a message from God to your own heart.

7. *I must approach the Word reverently.* I do not suggest that you come blindly, but I must remind you that the Bible does not yield its riches to the skeptic or the critic. Only by faith will it bring enrichment to your life. You can take a rose apart and study its component parts and yet miss entirely its beauty. Do not become discouraged with difficult passages, for they may unfold at subsequent readings or by comparison with other recognized versions. You will find, with a reverent attitude, rich veins of golden truth. You will discover that contradictions are only apparent.

> *Within that awful volume lies*
> *The mystery of mysteries.*

> *Happiest they of human race*
> *To whom their God has given grace*
> *To read, to fear, to hope, to pray,*
> *To lift the latch, and force the way;*
> *And better had they ne'er been born*
> *Who read to doubt, or read to scorn.*[1]

The fierce winds of criticism have blown upon the Word of God, but it is like the Irishman's stone fence. He lived in a region of high winds and it is said that he built a stone fence four feet high and six feet wide, for he said, "When the wind turns it over it will be higher than it was before."

8. *I must turn from its pages to prayer.* This is the proper conclusion for my reading. My prayer should be one of thanksgiving for God's message to me, one of praise for the Spirit's faithfulness to my heart, one of petition for courage to meet the new challenges He has given me, one of acknowledgment as to past failures, one of intercession for the needs of others, and one of gladness for the new sense of His presence.

What Shall I Read?

The leaves were still on the trees, late roses on the bushes, and zinnias yet tall, straight, and colorful in the backyard gardens when hordes of white visitors rushed to a resting place and to eventual oblivion. The snow had come so early and unexpectedly! Life is like that. Emergencies are not heralded and the coming of temptations and trials is not announced. We know that they will come eventually, but they usually surprise us. The Bible is a Refuge when the battle becomes hard and rough. More than that, it is Strength for the daily march, for in the quiet hour the Word gives us our "marching orders" for the day. The Bible, however, must be read that we might be prepared for the difficult hours. The

Psalmist said, "Thy word have I hid in mine heart, that I might not sin against thee" (Ps. 119:11).

I *must* read God's Word. As a young person or new Christian, where shall I begin? Before we suggest some starting points, let us give you one word of caution. Do not expect to master the Bible in a short time and do not be disturbed if much of it at first seems unwilling to yield its secrets. Keep reading and the time will come when you will feel as much at home in this Immortal Library of 66 books as you do in the company of your best friend. The following suggestions are given with those in mind who have read the Bible only casually or to whom it is an entirely new book.

1. *Start your reading with the New Testament.* Begin with the Gospel of Mark or of Luke, that you might get the story of Him who is the Supreme Person of human history. Read the Gospel of Mark, which records the preaching of "The Big Fisherman." Here you have a book of action, which is indicated by its key word "straightway," that occurs over 40 times in Mark's Gospel. It is a swift-moving record of the life of Jesus. The Gospel written by Luke, the physician, is also a good starting place. Here you have Paul's personal physician giving the finest historical record of the life of Christ. Turn then to the Book of Acts, where you have the record of the beginnings of the Christian Church. Do not take too great a portion at a time, but keep at it until you have finished these books. It is essential to know something about the life of Christ, the beginnings of the Church, and the conversion of St. Paul. Read then some of the shorter letters of Paul to the young churches. Go back and read then the Gospel of St. John, perhaps the favorite of all the New Testament books.

2. *Turn now to the Old Testament.* Start with Genesis, the book of beginnings. It is filled with human-interest stories. Go now to the great devotional literature of the Old Testament, the Psalms. Everyone who reads the Bible at all likes

the Psalms. You will find here many choice chapters. Any list would perhaps miss someone's favorite, but here are a few of the choice psalms:

Psalm 1—The Two Ways of Life
Psalm 19—Two Great Books, Nature and Scripture
Psalm 23—The Shepherd Psalm (perhaps the best loved of all)
Psalm 24—The Hymn of the King of Glory
Psalm 27—David's Song of Deliverance
Psalm 46—A Mighty Fortress, a Mighty Presence
Psalm 51—The Ageless Agony, a Prayer for All
Psalm 84—A Psalm of Peace
Psalm 90—Man's Frailty, Life's Brevity, and God's Eternity
Psalm 91—The Soul's Security
Psalm 100—The Doxology
Psalm 103—The Song of Gratitude, the Most Joyful Psalm
Psalm 107—The Great Psalm of Redemption
Psalm 116—An Expression of Genuine Thanksgiving
Psalm 119—A Little Bible in Itself

After the Psalms, turn to Proverbs and spend some time with those rich statements of wisdom; then to the choice chapters of the prophecy of Isaiah, such as: Isaiah 35, 40, 53, 55. From there you might turn to several of the shorter books such as Ruth or Jonah, and follow these with the large prophetical books.

3. *Read again those passages or chapter that helped you most.* There are some selections that help no matter how often they are read. The Word never wears out; it is ever new. While you are receiving help from the familiar paths, be looking for new trails to God's rich truth for your life. Don't get into a rut with your reading, avoiding everything but the familiar, for difficult passages sometimes can be mastered by repeated readings. Repetition does have great value. D. L. Moody has been quoted as saying, "My greatest spiritual ex-

perience was reading Ephesians through 47 times in a month."

4. *Read the stories of the Bible.* Everyone enjoys a story and the Bible has many of them. Here is a partial list from the Old and New Testaments:

Stories of the Old Testament

1.	The Creation and First Sin	Gen. 2:4—3:24
2.	The First Murder	Gen. 4:1-15
3.	The Flood	Gen. 6:1—9:17
4.	The Tower of Babel	Gen. 11:1-9
5.	The Destruction of Sodom and Gomorrah and of Lot's Wife	Gen. 19:1-28
6.	Abraham's Offering of Isaac	Gen. 22:1-19
7.	The Story of Jacob	Gen. 25:19—35:29
8.	The Story of Joseph	Genesis 37—50
9.	Moses in Egypt	Exodus 1—14
10.	Rahab, Red Cord, and Flax	Joshua 2
11.	Joshua, Military Strategist	Joshua 3; 6; 8
12.	The Defeat of Sisera	Josh. 4:4-24
13.	Gideon, Conqueror of the Philistines	Judg. 6:11—8:32
14.	The Story of Samson	Judg. 13:24—16:31
15.	The Story of Ruth	Ruth 1—4
16.	The Story of Samuel	1 Sam.1—3; 7—10; 12; 15—16:23
17.	Saul, the First King of the Hebrews	1 Sam. 8—11; 13; 15; 23:3-25, 31
18.	David, the Shepherd King	1 Sam. 16—27; 29—30:25 2 Sam. 9; 11; 12; 15:1-18; 18 1 Kings 1:1-31; 2:1-12
19.	King Solomon	1 Kings 1—11
20.	Elijah, the Great Prophet	1 Kings 17—19 2 Kings 1—2:15

21.	Elisha, His Successor	2 Kings 2:1-25; 4:8-37; 6; 13:14-21
22.	Naaman, the Leper	2 Kings 5
23.	Nehemiah	Nehemiah 1; 2; 4
24.	The Heroism of Esther	Esther 1:10—7:10
25.	Shadrach, Meshach, and Abednego	Daniel 3
26.	Belshazzar's Feast and the Handwriting on the Wall	Daniel 5
27.	Daniel in the Lions' Den	Daniel 6
28.	Jonah, the Reluctant Missionary	Jonah 1—4

Stories of the New Testament

1.	The Execution of John the Baptist by Herod	Matthew 3 Mark 1:1-11 Luke 3:1-20
2.	The Birth of Jesus	Matt. 1:18—2:15
3.	The Temptation of Jesus	Matt. 4:1-11 Mark 1:12-13 Luke 4:1-13
4.	The Sermon on the Mount	Matthew 5—7 Luke 6:20-49
5.	The Healing of a Leper	Matt. 8:1-4 Mark 1:40-45 Luke 5:12-16
6.	The Calming of the Tempest	Matt. 8:23-27 Mark 4:35-41 Luke 8:22-25
7.	The Man with the Palsy	Matt. 9:1-8 Mark 2:1-12 Luke 5:17-26
8.	The Daughter of Jairus and the Woman with an Issue	Matt. 9:18-26 Mark 5:21-43 Luke 8:40-56
9.	The Feeding of the Five Thousand	Matt. 14:13-23 Mark 6:30-46 Luke 9:10-17 John 6:1-15

10.	The Draught of Fishes	Luke 5:1-11
11.	The Widow's Son	Luke 7:11-17
12.	The Ten Lepers Cleansed	Luke 17:11-19
13.	The Raising of Lazarus	John 11:1-46
14.	The Sower	Matt. 13:1-23
		Mark 4:1-20
		Luke 8:1-15
15.	The Precious Pearl	Matt. 13:45-46
16.	The Unmerciful Servant	Matt. 18:23-35
17.	The Two Sons	Matt. 21:28-32
18.	The Marriage Feast	Matt. 22:1-14
		Luke 14:16-24
19.	The Ten Virgins	Matt. 25:1-13
20.	The Talents	Matt. 25:14-30
21.	The Good Samaritan	Luke 10:25-37
22.	The Rich Fool	Luke 12:16-21
23.	The Prodigal Son	Luke 15:11-32
24.	The Rich Man and Lazarus	Luke 16:19-31
25.	The Triumph of Jesus	Matt. 21:1-11
		Mark 11:1-11
		Luke 19:29-40
		John 12:12-19
26.	The Last Supper	Matt. 26:17-25
		Mark 14:12-26
		Luke 22:1-22
27.	The Agony of Jesus in Gethsemane	Matt. 26:36-46
		Mark 14:32-42
		Luke 22:39-46
28.	The Crucifixion of Jesus	Matt. 26:47—27:66
		Mark 14:43—15:47
		Luke 22:47—23:56
		John 18:19
29.	The Resurrection of Jesus	Matt. 28:1-10
		Mark 16
		Luke 24:1-12
		John 20
30.	The Ascension of Jesus	Acts 1:1-12
31.	The Pentecost	Acts 2:1-11
32.	Stephen, the First Martyr	Acts 6:5-15; 7:54-60
33.	Saul of Tarsus	Acts 9:1-32
34.	The Shipwreck of Paul	Acts 27—28:10

5. *Read the Bible consecutively.* It is valuable to read a book at a time. I do not necessarily mean always at one sitting. It is interesting, however, to note that 33 out of the 66 books of the Bible can be read in less than 1 hour. Then it is a good plan to read the Old or New Testament straight through.

6. *Read the whole Bible through.* Now that you have become familiar with this Immortal Library, you may want to read the entire Book. We need to do more than place as it were the microscope on a particular word or passage. It is vitally important that we take the telescope and catch a view of the entirety of God's unique revelation.

You can read the entire Bible through in a year, by reading three chapters each weekday and five on Sunday. By reading two chapters each day, you can complete the New Testament in less than 20 weeks. Seek, however, to get the great moral and spiritual lessons and do not read merely to keep a schedule. If your time is more limited than others, do not let this plan discourage you but spread your reading out over a longer period of time.

A leaflet *My Reading Record* is an aid to help you keep a record of your progress. The leaflet is prepared by and can be obtained from The New York International Bible Society, 450 Park Avenue, New York, NY 10022.

And Now a Challenge

Let us endeavor to be Bible readers and may the words of John Wesley help us in our noble effort.

Give Me the Book![2]

I am a creature of a day, passing through life as an arrow through the air. I am a spirit come from God, and returning to God; just hovering over the great gulf till a few moments hence I am no more seen! I drop into an unchangeable eternity!

I want to know one thing, the way to heaven: how to land safe on that happy shore. God Himself has condescended to teach the way; for this very end Jesus came from heaven. He hath written it down in a Book! Oh, give me that Book! At any price, give me the Book of God! I have it. Here is knowledge enough for me. Let me be a HOMO UNIUS LIBRI *("man of one book").*

Here then I am, far from the busy ways of men. I sit down lone; only God is here. In His Presence I open, I read this Book, for this end, to find the way to heaven. Is there a doubt concerning the meaning of what I read? Does anything appear dark or intricate? I lift up my heart to the Father of lights. Lord, is it not Thy Word: "If any . . . lack wisdom, let him ask of God, that giveth . . . liberally and upbraideth not." "If any will to do his will, he shall know." I am willing to do; let me know Thy will.

I then search after and consider parallel passages of Scripture, "comparing spiritual things with spiritual." I meditate thereon with all the attention and earnestness of which my mind is capable. If any doubt still remains, I consult those who are experienced in the things of God, and then the writings whereby, being dead, they speak. And what I learn, that I teach.

3

Simple Methods for Bible Study

Bible study is more than Bible reading. Bible reading may be more extensive and Bible study more intensive. The earlier in life or in Christian experience that you begin to study the Word, the richer your life will become from the accumulating dividends of the hours and hard work invested in studying life's supreme Guidebook. Paul, that great apostle, wrote thus to Timothy, his son in the faith, "Study to shew thyself approved unto God, a workman that needeth not to be ashamed, rightly dividing the word of truth" (2 Tim. 2:15). Both Dr. A. T. Pierson and Dr. W. H. Griffith Thomas use the following terms in their reference to the study of the Word: *search, meditate,* and *compare.* God will give the secrets of His Book to you only if you are patient, persistent, and industrious. With purposeful effort and with the Holy Spirit as your Teacher, the Bible can become your very own.

The simple methods suggested in this chapter are given with a prayer that some of them may be of special blessing to you in your effort to do effective studying of the Word and thus make the Bible really yours. Have a definite plan and sometimes vary your methods. Do not set your goal too high nor be satisfied with too little. And remember that your efforts are spent that the Bible might become a practical Guide for the life that God has given to you.

The Book Method

Each book in this Immortal Library has its contribution to make to the whole. Do not expect to come to an understanding of the entire Library in a short time. It will take years for a comprehensive study of the Bible. We are merely suggesting here ways to begin your study.

Dr. James M. Gray, former president of Moody Bible Institute and author of *Commentary on the Bible* and *Synthetic Bible Studies,* describes his method of Bible study in his book *How to Master the English Bible.* He simply read and reread a book until he felt that he had a thorough understanding of it and then began the same practice with the next book until he had gone through the entire Bible. He started with Genesis and continued through the Library. That was the method of an outstanding Bible scholar.

As a young person or new Christian, you may feel that Dr. Gray's method is too large an assignment. If so, I suggest that you select from the Library those books with which you would like to begin. Here are 10 suggestions:

1. Genesis—The Book of Beginnings
2. Ruth—A great story and a literary gem
3. Isaiah—The great major prophecy
4. Jonah—Judgment and repentance
5. The Gospel of John—The Son of God
6. The Acts of the Apostles—The vital link between the Gospels and the Epistles; the beginnings of the Church
7. Epistle to the Romans—According to Luther, "The chief book of the New Testament"
8. Ephesians—In heavenly places with Christ
9. Hebrews—The supremacy of Christ
10. The Revelation—Christ and the things to come

As you make a study of a book, keep these things in mind.

1. Its purpose

2. Its story
3. The main events
4. The chief character or characters
5. The author and the people to whom it was written
6. The main message of the book
7. Make a note of the spiritual lessons you discovered

THE CHAPTER METHOD

We believe in the inspiration of the Word in its totality. Every chapter, however, will not yield the same richness of spiritual truth for you. There is no chapter without spiritual worth but some will be much more rewarding than others. Time spent with the favorite chapters will be very beneficial to you.

To help you get started, let me suggest 25 great chapters that you should study.

1. Genesis 1
2. Exodus 20
3. Psalm 23
4. Isaiah 35
5. Isaiah 55
6. Matthew 5
7. Matthew 6
8. Matthew 7
9. Mark 11
10. Luke 15
11. John 1
12. John 3
13. John 14
14. John 15
15. John 17
16. Acts 2
17. Acts 12
18. Romans 12
19. 1 Corinthians 13
20. Ephesians 6
21. Philippians 2
22. Hebrews 11
23. Revelation 1
24. Revelation 5
25. Revelation 21

Here are 10 questions that you may ask about each chapter. They are suggested to us by Miss Grace Saxe and listed by Dr. Wilbur M. Smith in *Profitable Bible Study*.[1]

1. What is the principal subject of this chapter?
2. What is the leading lesson of this chapter?
3. Which is the best verse in this chapter?

4. Who are the principal persons in this chapter?
5. What does the chapter teach concerning Christ?
6. Is there, in this chapter, any example for me to follow?
7. Is there, in this chapter, any error for me to avoid?
8. Is there, in this chapter, any duty for me to perform?
9. Is there, in this chapter, any promise for me to claim?
10. Is there, in this chapter, any prayer for me to echo?

Sometimes you may wish to attempt an outline of the chapter you are studying. Some chapters are easier to outline than others. An outline does help in the study of a chapter. For example, the three sections of John 17, "The Prayer of the Great High Priest," are helpful in the understanding of the chapter.

1. The High Priest prays for himself (vv. 1-5).
2. The High Priest prays for His disciples (vv. 6-19).
3. The High Priest prays for His Church (vv. 20-26).

THE BIOGRAPHICAL METHOD

There are nearly 3,000 people mentioned in the Bible. Someone has estimated the number of persons at 2,930. In some cases only the name is mentioned, while the biographies of others occupy a large portion of the Word. One of the most fruitful approaches to Bible study is that of getting acquainted with the people. The people will live again for you, and the story of their trials and triumphs has much to contribute to your own life. In fact, no one can master the Bible and not become acquainted with those who have so much to do with it all.

For a number of years Dr. Oscar F. Reed made it a practice to preach a series of messages on biblical characters on Sunday evenings during the summer months. He says that they have always increased attendance and have been the means of soul winning. Here is one of the sermon series used by Dr. Reed. Can you identify the characters?

WHO WERE THEY?[2]

1. He Played with Extinction
2. His Soul Was a Soul of Iron
3. This Woman—a Leader of Men
4. The Loneliest Man in History
5. He Was Inspired of God to Do the Impossible
6. Prehensile at Birth
7. A Young Man Who Said No
8. They Laughed at His Faith
9. Beautiful—but Not Dumb
10. Born in Secret—Buried by God
11. He Sensed the Futility of External Religion

Have you guessed them all? Check your list with the answers given in the notes at the end of the book.

You may be interested in studying the various groups of characters. Here are a few suggestions:

1. The Rogues (great sinners) of the Bible
2. The Famous Men of the Bible
3. The Famous Women of the Bible
4. The Great Soldiers of the Bible
5. The Little-known People of the Bible
6. The Friends of Jesus
7. The Enemies of the Master
8. The Outstanding Boys and Girls of the Bible
9. The Great Servants of the Bible
10. The Failures of the Bible

Above all, in acquainting yourself with the personalities of the Bible, seek to learn those lessons that have meaning for our time as well as theirs. Take note of how sin and righteousness worked in their lives and gain those lessons that will be profitable to us.

THE WORD OR PHRASE METHOD

Words are the vehicles in God's convoy of revelation. All of them have their place, but some are more highly significant than others. There are approximately 6,000 different English words that appear in the Authorized Version of the Bible. A study of the important words of the Bible will be most rewarding and yield many riches. For example, spend time in your study of such words as faith, grace, hope, love, life, light, joy, know, abide, believe, and now.

Essential in this approach to the wealth of God's Word is a complete concordance. Let me suggest these three: Cruden's, Strong's, and Young's. With your concordance as your companion volume, make a word study and come to know the significant words in their various settings. Let me suggest that you give some attention to the following:

In Genesis—beginning
In Joshua—possess or possessions
In the Psalms—blessed
In Isaiah—salvation
In Malachi—wherein and rob
In Mark—straightway
In the Gospel of John and the Epistles of John—life, light, love, and believe
In Ephesians—together and one
In Hebrews—better
In 1 and 2 Peter—suffering and precious
In Revelation—overcome

The possibilities in this approach are almost limitless. The word *come* is a great study. Here are a few of the interesting words of Jesus:

The "excepts" of Jesus.
The "verilys" of Jesus.
The "amens" of Jesus.

Let us give attention also to some of the phrases that make most interesting study. Here again the field is large and we can list only a few.

1. The "Fear nots" of Isaiah
    a. Isa. 41:10-14

  b. Isa. 43:1-7
  c. Isa. 44:1-5
  d. Isa. 54:4-17
2. The "I ams" of Christ
  a. "I am from above"—John 8:23
  b. "I am not of this world"—John 8:23
  c. "I am the bread of life"—John 6:35
  d. "I am the light of the world"—John 8:12
  e. "Before Abraham was, I am"—John 8:58
  f. "I am the door"—John 10:9
  g. "I am the good shepherd"—John 10:11
  h. "I am the resurrection, and the life"—John 11:25
  i. "I am the way, the truth, and the life"—John 14:6
  j. "I am the true vine"—John 15:1
  k. "I am the Alpha and Omega"—Rev. 1:8, 11
  l. "I am he that liveth"—Rev. 1:18
  m. "I am the bright and morning star"—Rev. 22:16
3. "Let us" in Hebrews
  a. Let us fear—4:1
  b. Let us enter into His rest—4:11
  c. Let us hold fast—4:14
  d. Let us come with our needs—4:16
  e. Let us go on—6:1
  f. Let us draw nigh—10:19-22
  g. Let us hold fast without wavering—10:23
  h. Let us assist others to faith—10:24, 25
  i. Let us run the race—12:1
  j. Let us receive—12:28
  k. Let us go forth—13:12-14
  l. Let us give praise and render service—13:15, 16
4. There are eight important appearances of "We know" in the First Epistle of John. They are: 2:29; 5:18; 3:2; 3:5; 3:14; 3:24; 5:13; and 5:15.

Many other studies of this nature can be made. Here are a few additional suggestions:

"This man"
"One thing"
"Follow me"
"If any man"

"Be of good cheer"
"All things"

THE TOPICAL METHOD

This approach has many possibilities and will indeed be most rewarding. It is difficult to know where to begin when so many interesting subjects clamor for attention. For example, there are at least 75 *great poems* in the Bible. As a starting point, let us suggest just 15:

1. Moses' Song of Deliverance—Exod. 15:1-19
2. The Hymn of Deborah—Judg. 5:1-31
3. The Song of Hannah—1 Sam. 2:1-10
4. The Prayer of David—2 Sam. 7:18-29
5. The Prayer of Solomon—1 Kings 8:22-61
6. The Wolf and the Lamb—Isa. 11:1-9
7. Have You Not Known?—Isaiah 40
8. Beauty for Ashes—Isa. 61:1-6
9. The Foxes Walk—Lamentations 5
10. Swords into Plowshares—Mic. 4:1-5
11. The Hills Melt—Nah. 1:2-7
12. The Hymn of Mary—Luke 1:46-55
13. The Benediction of Simeon—Luke 2:29-32
14. Where Is the Victory?—1 Corinthians 15
15. Alpha and Omega—Rev. 21:1-7

(The Bible student wishing to follow a topical plan of study should have a copy of *A Topical Text Book,* by R. A. Torrey.)

Another most profitable study is that of the *prayers of the Bible.* There are over 100 great prayers in the Bible. Let me suggest that you begin with the prayers of St. Paul. Here are 14 of them:

1. 1 Thess. 3:12-13
2. 1 Thess. 5:23-24
3. 2 Thess. 1:11-12
4. 2 Thess. 2:16-17

5. 2 Thess. 3:5
6. 2 Thess. 3:16
7. 2 Cor. 13:7-9
8. Rom. 15:5-6
9. Rom. 15:13
10. Col. 1:9-14
11. Col. 2:1-4
12. Eph. 1:15-21
13. Eph. 3:14-21
14. Phil. 1:9-11

You may wish to study the *water scenes* of the Bible. Here are a few of them:

1. Moses in the bulrushes
2. Elijah at the Brook Cherith
3. Noah and the flood
4. Jonah and the trip to Tarshish
5. General Naaman at muddy Jordan
6. Israel at the Red Sea
7. The baptism of Jesus at Jordan
8. Christ stilling the tempest
9. Peter walking on the water
10. Christ teaching from a boat
11. Paul shipwrecked
12. The impotent man at Bethesda

There are so many suitable topics for Bible study. Let us suggest only a few more:

1. The Doctrines of the Bible
2. The Night Scenes of the Bible
3. The Mountain Scenes of the Bible
4. The Gardens of God's Book
5. The Cities, the Occupations, and the "Small Things"
6. The Prophecies Concerning Christ
7. The Great Conversions
8. The Parables and Miracles of Christ
9. Questions That Jesus Asked
10. Questions Asked Jesus
11. The Invitations of Jesus
12. The Revivals of the Bible

The Whole Story Method

You will want to have an understanding of *the story of the Bible* as well as the stories of the Bible. Study the Bible as a whole with these books for your guides.

1. *Exploring the Old Testament,* edited by W. T. Purkiser.[3]
2. *Exploring the New Testament,* edited by Ralph Earle.[4]

Go through these with an open Bible and the results will be most gratifying. Other similar aids may also be obtained.

Comparison of Translations Method

There are a number of versions of the Bible or New Testament available today that can be of assistance to you. Particularly are they of value in bringing the message of the Bible in the language of today. They can be of value also in understanding those passages that are not clear. By comparing the King James Version with another version or with several other versions, these passages quite frequently become clear.

Many new modern language versions of the Bible have appeared in recent years. The *New International Version* is one of the latest and most widely used of these translations. Other versions of the Bible in modern English include the following:

> *The Bible—An American Translation,* by J. M. Powis Smith and Edgar J. Goodspeed
> *The Bible—A New Translation,* by James Moffatt
> *The Berkeley Version,* by Gerritt Verkuyl
> The *Revised Standard Version*
> The *New English Bible*
> *The Living Bible*
> The *New American Standard Bible*
> The *Amplified Bible*
> *Good News Bible, Today's English Version*

A number of helpful translations of the New Testament are available today. You will find the following very stimulating in Bible study:

The New Testament in Modern English, by J. B. Phillips
The New Testament in Modern Speech, by Richard F. Weymouth
The New Testament, by Charles B. Williams

The Commentary Method

After you have used other methods of studying the Word, it will be profitable to turn to some of the commentaries and, with an open Bible, let them assist you in finding the meaning and depths of truth that you have yet been unable to discover. They cannot be a substitute for other methods of direct Bible study. The outstanding commentaries, however, are the result of a lifetime of study on the part of consecrated men, and their expositions and interpretations do have great value. Study them to find help on that passage, verse, or chapter that has seemed a bit difficult to you. Even in this method of study do not take every word of any particular commentator as final. Here too, seek the guidance of the Holy Spirit. Bible scholars may differ, but the Holy Spirit can help you to come to an answer that will be satisfying to you.

If you are going to make a thorough study of the Word with these helps, you ought to have several commentaries, so that you can compare the results of the findings of good men.

The Verse Method

Not every verse has the same value for our devotional study, but there are verses without number that will bring blessing to us as we study them and meditate upon them. Some years ago I heard Dr. Harry E. Jessop preach on this verse, "Nay, in all these things we are more than conquerors through him that loved us" (Rom. 8:37). The outline he suggested has stayed with me.

The Situation—"In all these things"

The Declaration—"We are more than conquerors"

The Explanation—"Through him that loved us"

Every verse of scripture that we study will not fall into simple and clear outline. But a careful study of individual verses will yield many riches.

THE PARAGRAPH OR PASSAGE METHOD

There are certain portions of God's Word that have already fastened themselves upon you if you have been a reader or student of the Bible at all. Every paragraph or passage with a predominant message or thought will not be equally important to you. There are some that would merit a great amount of study. There is one paragraph that has never lost its thrill for me. It is Eph. 3:14-21.

Let me suggest that in your study of paragraphs you give time to those portions that will challenge you to high and holy living. Here are a few examples: 2 Pet. 2:5-9; Gal. 5:22-26; the Beatitudes; 1 Corinthians 13; Paul's prayers, and the parables of Jesus. You can never exhaust the wealth of these portions.

THE GEOGRAPHICAL METHOD

The Bible will mean more to you if you can gain some understanding of the places of which it speaks. A map of Jerusalem and of the Holy Land is of value. With the aid of a Bible atlas study the footprints of Jesus and the missionary journeys of St. Paul. Know something of those familiar rivers, mountains, and towns of the Bible. For this study a manual of biblical geography, a Bible encyclopedia, or a Bible dictionary will be of real help. Not everyone can take a trip to the Holy Land. Even then a study of the geography of the Bible would be the essential preparation. Everyone can know something about the places often mentioned in the Word of God, and this acquaintance will make the Bible live.

THE DEPTH METHOD

In depth Bible study the approach is intensely personal. The central idea is to search the same portion of scripture for a period of time to discover its message in terms of our lives today. The significant question for the student is: What does this passage say to me? The Bible becomes meaningful as we ask the Holy Spirit to show us new truth or to throw new light on an old truth.

The following depth study techniques may be helpful:

1. Read and reread the selected passage silently and thoughtfully.

2. Read the passage aloud, either to others at family worship or to yourself in your personal devotions.

3. Write down your thoughts and questions. Discuss these at family worship or with a close friend.

4. Underline in your Bible significant words, phrases, or a favorite verse in the passage.

5. Try to clear up the meaning of obscure phrases or words by reading the passage in one or more of the modern language versions.

6. Consult such works of experienced and devout Bible scholars as a Bible commentary, a Bible atlas, a Bible dictionary, a complete concordance, or other Bible reference books.

7. Ask God to help you apply the message of this passage to your daily life.

THE CENTRAL PERSONALITY METHOD

Above all, let us study the Word of God to know more about Jesus Christ. In the Old Testament we see Him in the theophanies, in the sacrificial offerings, in the types and shadows, in the symbolism of the Tabernacle and Temple, and in the mighty message of the prophets. In the New Testament we behold His glory, "the glory as of the only begotten of the Father, full of grace and truth" (John 1:14). Dr. George F. Pentecost said, "Christ and the Scriptures are inseparable —Revelation culminates in Him. Without Him the Bible would be a meaningless book; unintelligible in its history, in its types and ceremonials, and in its prophecy . . . From the time when God announced in the Garden of Eden that the seed of the woman should bruise the serpent's head (Gen. 3:15) until the time when John cried, in response to the apocalyptic vision, 'Even so, come, Lord Jesus' (Rev. 22:20), He is seen to be the central fact and figure of the Book. As the sun casts a shadow before an advancing body, so Jesus, who was the Lamb slain from the foundation of the world, . . . cast the long line of typical and ceremonial shadows before Him."[5]

A Final Tribute to the Word

"With the Holy Spirit for my guide, I entered this wonderful temple that we call Christianty. I entered through the portico of Genesis and walked down through the Old Testament's art gallery, where I saw the portraits of Joseph, Jacob, Daniel, Moses, Isaiah, Solomon and David hanging on the wall; I entered the music room of the Psalms and the Spirit of God struck the keyboard of my nature until it seemed to me that every reed and pipe in God's great organ of nature responded to the harp of David, and the charm of King Solomon in his moods.

"I walked into the business house of Proverbs.

"I walked into the observatory of the prophets and there saw photographs of various sizes, some pointing to far-off stars or events—all concentrated upon one great Star which was to rise as an atonement for sin.

"Then I went into the audience room of the King of Kings, and got a vision from four different points—from Matthew, Mark, Luke, and John. I went into the correspondence room, and saw Peter, James, Paul and Jude, penning their epistles to the world. I went into the Acts of the Apostles and saw the Holy Spirit forming the Holy Church, and then I walked into the throne room and saw a door at the foot of a tower and, going up, I saw One standing there, fair as the morning, Jesus Christ, the Son of God, and I found this truest friend that man ever knew; when all were false I found Him true.

"In teaching me the way of life, the Bible has taught me the way to live, it taught me how to die."[6]

Part II

THY WORD IN MY HEART

A Scripture Memorization Manual

Wherewithal shall a young man cleanse his way? by taking heed thereto according to thy word.

With my whole heart have I sought thee; O let me not wander from thy comandments.

Thy word have I hid in mine heart, that I might not sin against thee.

Blessed art thou, O Lord: teach me thy statutes.

With my lips have I declared all the judgments of thy mouth.

I have rejoiced in the way of thy testimonies, as much as in all riches.

I will meditate in thy precepts, and have respect unto thy ways.

I will delight myself in thy statutes: I will not forget thy word (Ps. 119:9-16).

In Westminster Abbey, at the coronation of Queen Elizabeth, the moderator of the Church of Scotland presented Her Majesty with a copy of the Bible, saying to the Queen in the act of presentation, "This is the most valuable thing the world affords."

The Bible Is—

The charter of all true liberty
The forerunner of all civilization
The molder of institutions and governments
The fashioner of law
The secret of national progress
The guide of history
The ornament and mainspring of literature
The inspiration of philosophies
The textbook of ethics
The light of the intellect
The soul of all strong heart life
The illuminator of darkness
The foe of superstition
The enemy of oppression
The uprooter of sin
The comfort in sorrow
The strength in weakness
The pathway in perplexity
The escape from temptation
The steadier in the day of power
The embodiment of lofty ideals
The begetter of life
The promise of the future
The star of death's night
The revealer of God
The guide and hope and the inspiration of man

—BISHOP WILLIAM F. ANDERSON

On Memorizing the Scriptures

Dr. Wilfred T. Grenfell, missionary in Labrador, said many years ago: "Most gladly I give the testimony of my experience concerning the memorizing of Scripture. To me it has been an unfailing help in doubt, anxiety, sorrow and all the countless vicissitudes and problems of life. I believe in it enough to have devoted many, many hours to stowing away passages where I can neither leave them behind me nor be unable to get at them. Facing death alone on a floating piece of ice on a freezing ocean, the comradeship it [the Scripture] afforded me supplied all I needed. With my whole soul I commend to others the giving of some little time each day to secure the immense returns Scripture memorization insures."

Foreword

This section on values and methods has been prepared to assist the Christian to memorize the scriptures. However, the main thing is to get started in the all-important expedition. As a young Christian or possibly a new convert you must make the Word of God important in your life. There is no better way to do this than to commit portions of it to memory. And above all, begin now. Do not put it off as a good resolution to begin next month or next year. Make plans to start in today. Begin to memorize as you read this booklet. Practice the methods given upon verses which you are learning.

To assist you in the overall task, a Memory Course has been outlined. This is a topical plan, bringing to your attention significant scriptures dealing with several very important phases of your Christian life. The plan in full will be presented in Chapter 2. But in order that you might have something with which to begin, 12 verses out of this plan have been selected, which are known as Basic Memory Verses. Of these, 6 are for personal strength as you move out into the Christian life and 6 are to assist you in witnessing to others. As a young Christian you must grow in strength and grace through the Word and you must also know the Word in telling others of the Savior.

Basic Memory Verses

1. The Word

"As newborn babes, desire the sincere milk of the word, that ye may grow thereby: if so be ye have tasted that the Lord is gracious" (1 Pet. 2:2-3).

2. Witnessing

"And they overcame him by the blood of the Lamb, and by the word of their testimony; and they loved not their lives unto the death" (Rev. 12:11).

3. Assurance

"And this is the record, that God hath given to us eternal life, and this life is in his Son" (1 John 5:11).

4. Obedience

"And being made perfect, he became the author of eternal salvation unto all them that obey him" (Heb. 5:9).

5. Prayer

"Hitherto have ye asked nothing in my name: ask, and ye shall receive, that your joy may be full" (John 16:24).

6. Temptation

"There hath no temptation taken you but such as is common to man; but God is faithful, who will not suffer you to be tempted above that ye are able; but will with the temptation also make a way to escape, that ye may be able to bear it" (1 Cor. 10:13).

7. Fact of Sin

"For all have sinned, and come short of the glory of God" (Rom. 3:23).

8. Penalty of Sin

"For the wages of sin is death; but the gift of God is eternal life through Jesus Christ our Lord" (Rom. 6:23).

9. Savior from Sin

"But God commendeth his love toward us, in that, while we were yet sinners, Christ died for us" (Rom. 5:8).

10. Remedy for Sin

"In whom we have redemption through his blood, the forgiveness of sins, according to the riches of his grace" (Eph. 1:7).

11. Repentance of Sin

"Repent ye therefore, and be converted, that your sins may be blotted out, when the times of refreshing shall come from the presence of the Lord" (Acts 3:19).

12. Believing for Salvation

"But as many as received him, to them gave he power to become the sons of God, even to them that believe on his name" (John 1:12).

Some Pointers

Here are some starting points that will help you as you move out into this grand adventure of scripture memorization.

1. Master the 12 Basic Memory Verses listed above.

2. Memorize the verses *accurately*. Quality and not quantity is the goal. A verse is not memorized until you can quote it without any mistake. Do your work thoroughly and it will surely be more lasting.

3. State the reference *before* and *after* you quote the verse. This method will enable you to fix those references in your mind.

4. After you have mastered the Basic Memory Verse, go on to complete the Beginner's Memory Course.

5. Master each course before you go on to the next.

6. Review constantly the verses you have learned even as you are working on the new course.

7. Don't wait until you have finished reading this book. Take your Bible and go to work.

4

Memorizing the Scriptures

One of the bulwarks to faith and one of the greatest encouragements to the Christian life is the memorization of the scriptures. Too many times we have left this phase of Bible study to the boys and girls of the Sunday School. As young people and as new Christians we should plan, as one of our projects for the days ahead, systematically to memorize the Word of God. Let us hide the Word in our hearts in a practical and satisfactory way. Verses of the Word stored in our memories are both offensive and defensive weapons in time of need.

VALUES OF MEMORIZATION

It should not be necessary to call our attention to the values and importance of scripture memorization. But just to refresh our minds let us notice a few of these. We should memorize:

1. *To combat temptation.* It is noteworthy that Jesus successfully combated the devil in His hour of great temptation by quotations from the Word. The weapon that wins in the hour of extreme testing is the Word of God. The verses most applicable came to the mind and lips of Jesus. No doubt, in a greater sense than it was said of Timothy, Jesus from a child

had known the Holy Scriptures. We, too, will find that the Word will be a source of victory to us in our times of temptation. But, if we do not *know* the Word, we cannot use it.

2. *To help us in the absence of the printed Word.* Most of us are so situated that a Bible is nearly always available to us. But that may not always be so. A serviceman wrote from Korea that he was grateful a thousand times for the scriptures he had memorized, for much of the time because of battle conditions he could not read his Bible. Surely a soldier in combat would find the greatest of consolation out of such words as these: "For I am persuaded, that neither death, nor life, nor angels, nor principalities, nor powers, nor things present, nor things to come, nor height, nor depth, nor any other creature, shall be able to separate us from the love of God, which is in Christ Jesus our Lord" (Rom. 8:38-39).

It is good to file the rich portions of the Bible away in a place where neither circumstances nor evil men can take them away from us. The day could come when we would be put in jail for reading the Bible. Then those who have memorized portions of it will still have His Word.

3. *To give confidence in facing doctrinal discussions.* Not infrequently we come up against those who interpret the Scriptures differently from what we do. Perhaps they hold their position strongly and back it up with frequent quotations from the Bible. Are they right or wrong? Can we find the flaws in their arguments? Can we correctly state our position as taught by the Word? We can if we know the Word. And knowing the Word will give us confidence and assurance and faith.

4. *To provide us a tool in personal work.* People are not so much interested in our opinions about salvation as they are in what the Word of God says. It is difficult for the Christian to do an efficient task of soul winning if he is not acquainted with the Bible. The Word is the source of the promises of

God. The Christian worker should have a working knowledge of these promises which relate to salvation. The "Thus saith the Lord" is very important in pointing people to God.

5. *To build spiritual fiber.* Christian character is built; it does not evolve overnight. The structural steel of that character is the Word of God. The Christian who fails to build the facts, the spirit, the precepts, the principles, the strength of the Bible into his life is weak and shaky. It is noteworthy that the great men and women of the Church have been those who have made the significant portions of the Bible a part of the warp and woof of their lives. It is amazing how fast a person grows in spiritual things as he begins to make portions of God's Word his very own.

May every one of us feel the challenge to memorize the scriptures, purposefully, diligently, consistently, aggressively. And let us begin now!

SOME PRACTICAL SUGGESTIONS

1. *Your plan must be workable.* It may be possible for some to memorize a verse or two a day. I think, however, for most people it would be better to adopt the plan of a "verse a week" and carry through with it than to attempt too large an assignment. If every professed Christian and church member would fix in his memory a verse of Scripture every week, we could look for a great spiritual awakening.

2. *Memorize regularly.* We will accomplish more if we have a system and memorize regularly. Many verses can be learned if we would use a few leisure moments each day. It is not imperative that we set aside a definite time of the day for memory work. Even in walking or riding to or from work or school, the Word of God can be stored in our memory. Let us invest our spare moments memorizing God's Word.

3. *Use your favorite translation for memorizing.* We are privileged today to have available a variety of valuable trans-

lations. Some, of course, will want to use the familiar King James Version for memorizing. Others will prefer using their favorite modern translation. Whatever version you use, make it a practice to memorize often the Word of God.

4. *Remember that memorizing is no easy matter.* What is there in life that is worthwhile that does not have a price connected with it? Work hard, be persistent and patient in this noble endeavor. Someone has said that "genius is 90 percent perspiration and 10 percent inspiration." If you have never tried memorizing before, do not permit your first efforts to discourage you. A new job or position is difficult at first. Be determined to succeed and you will. At first you may not be so happy about your task as you will be if you keep up the good work. Satan will try to thwart the beginning efforts of the young person or new Christian, for he knows the value of the memorized Word. Don't be defeated in the beginning stages of a systematic effort to memorize the scriptures.

5. *Ask the Holy Spirit to help you.* The Spirit of the living God will aid you in fixing the Word in your memory. Depend on the Holy Spirit to give you guidance in the selection of the passages that will have a very practical future use. Pray as you memorize. Ask the Holy Spirit to help you in the use of the scriptures. Use the Word to give guidance to the unsaved, to help those who are in need of forgiveness, to encourage those whose cares are weighing them down, to solace those in sorrow, to assist those who are facing difficult problems, to give light to those who need to make a full and complete consecration, to show the way to those who would be holy in heart and life, and to dispel the fears of those who face the setting of life's sun. We must depend on the Spirit to help us to utilize those scriptures we have stored in our memories.

6. *Mark memorized portions in your Bible.* Make the markings of your Bible meaningful. You may have a special plan for marking your Bible, noting passages that have

blessed or helped you in your reading, passages that have been used as texts in sermons you have heard, or passages that have been special areas of study. In addition, however, there is value in marking the verses you have memorized. Use a separate color for these passages; then every time you read or study your Bible they will stand out and this will help in making them a very meaningful part of your life.

LAWS OF EFFECTIVE MEMORIZATION

There are certain laws of the human mind that, if followed, will enable one to memorize much more quickly and much more effectively. Memorization is not the great mystery that some would believe it to be. Memorization is not reserved alone for those who retain mental images more readily than others. True, some memorize more quickly and more permanently than do others. However, to everyone who will set himself to the task, amazing results will be achieved. Here are a few of the basic principles that should be observed. They are all based upon the three important factors in the process of creating lasting memory images:

a. Acquiring the image.

b. Retaining the image.

c. Recalling the image.

1. *Concentrate on what you are learning.* Concentration is one of the vital laws of memorization. It is the instrument that impresses experience and data deeply upon the mind. Lasting impressions are not made through an oscillation of the mind that touches lightly upon many things. Hence, you must study the scriptures with undivided attention and with the idea in mind that you are going to remember. You must learn to give diligent attention to the passage before you and, driving out the matters that struggle to claim your thoughts, focus the mind to learn. If you allow the scriptures to make

firm and definite lines upon the mind, they will not easily be erased.

Concentration and interest go hand in hand. It is most difficult to concentrate upon something in which you have no interest. Hence, sufficient interest will go far in helping you conquer the battle of concentration. As a Christian, you should be vitally interested in the Word of God and vitally interested in making it your own.

Every person can memorize portions of the Word if he is interested and if he goes about the task systematically and seriously. Interest is a basic principle in the learning process. Many people excuse themselves from memorizing God's Word on the basis of having a "poor memory." That is the telltale of a lack of genuine interest in committing to memory the treasures of the Book.

2. *Apply the principles of association.* According to the psychologists, man learns by associating the new with the old, the strange with the familiar. It is therefore helpful to use existing similarities as an aid to memorizing. The use of a series of verses where coincidences occur helps in retaining all of them—for example, the "3:16s of the Bible." See Proverbs, Malachi, Luke, John, Acts, 1 Corinthians, Colossians, 1 and 2 Timothy. Caution should be exercised in the use of artificial devices as aids to memorization. Any device that does not practically aid you in recalling should be discarded, for it is not a system that is important. The scaffold is only for the purpose of constructing the building.

Look for associations and use them. There are many possibilities of associations. Fixed in my memory is the identity of the 84th psalm due to its use in testimony by a very godly man. A great sermon stamped the 24th psalm upon my memory. Sunday School teachers often use simple mnemonics. For example, my teacher taught me the names and orders of the Gospels in this manner:

Matthew, Mark, Luke, and John—
Saddle your horse and travel on.

One of the major memory aids is association. There is:

(1) Association by logical connection.
(2) Association by similarity.
(3) Association by contrast.
(4) Association by simultaneous occurrence.

These principles of association may be applied to scripture memorization. For example, above we have noted the similarity of references in the "3:16s of the Bible." In the first psalm we have association by contrast. Let us look at the psalm, which depicts the two ways of life:

(1) Verses 1-3, The godly man prospers.
(2) Verses 4-6, The ungodly man perishes.

It is valuable to learn the references. There is much value in knowing the book, chapter, and verse of a quotation. If you memorize the reference, you can always locate the scripture quoted. A reference may stick with you and help locate the verse or passage that needs to be reviewed. In personal evangelism it is of much importance to point the one with whom you are dealing to the place in the Word where you have found such vital truth.

It is also valuable to relate the particular verse to the passage as a whole. Some may do their learning bit by bit. They may take a line or a phrase at a time, but a passage is remembered much better and for a longer period of time if it is learned as a whole. The piecemeal method is quite mechanical, while the method of understanding the entire portion gives a far better structure for lasting mental images. Read the verse, passage, or chapter over and over again. By repeated reading the portion can become so familiar that, almost before you are aware of it, it will be firmly fixed in your memory.

This method of familiarizing yourself with the whole portion emphasizes the main ideas and provides an adequate foundation for the work of more deliberate memorizing. Main ideas begin to link themselves together and an understanding of the entire passage is gained. The longer the passage, the more frequently it should be read in its entirety.

3. *Do your memorizing thoroughly.* Work well done is the best done. You are not on a Bible-memorizing marathon. Quality is to be desired above quantity and speed. Learn the verse or passage correctly and then you will be able to quote it properly. It may seem that you are not accomplishing much and that you are going too slowly, but master each verse or passage before you go on to the next. Go over what you have committed to memory and review it often.

Seek to understand the scriptures to be memorized. It is important to know what a passage means as well as what it says. To grasp the meaning is an aid to remembering the words. Read the verse, passage, or chapter over to discover its meaning and to gain the total picture. Meditate upon it in a quiet hour. Usually there is a dominant thought in the portion. Faithfulness in reading and studying the Word of God is a step toward effective memorization. That which you read often and understand will be remembered much easier than a mere jumble of words.

Learn the gradual way. Cramming is not the best way to learn. If you are going to give a reading or recite some scripture, do not wait until a day or two before the time, to start memorizing. Spread the memorizing period over as many days as possible. The best plan is to begin as soon as you know that you are to give the reading or recitation. A number of short periods of work on a passage will produce greater results than too long a stretch at one time.

Use every possible means of getting the particular passage impressed upon your mind.

Read it again and again. Through the "eye gate" come the strongest impressions. Read it until you can without the aid of the Bible or scripture card "see" the passage in print.

Write it out. The process of writing a phrase will impress it upon the mind. With the shorter verses or passages, write them over and over.

Read it aloud or have someone else read it to you. Always pronounce the words clearly and give each sentence full expression. Neither hurry nor slur the words. Avoid the mechanical and endeavor to keep the meaning of the verse or passage always clearly before you.

Have a verbal checkup. This plan will let you know how well you are getting along and will also encourage you to do your work thoroughly. It will also be a means perhaps of encouraging others to get started and will be a means of blessing to those to whom you repeat the Word.

4. *Review, review, review, review.* Review is imperative in memorization. The measure of retention when such review is used is amazing. William James, the noted American psychologist, relearned some poems he had memorized 40 years previously and found evidence of some retention after this long-time lapse. But the rate of forgetting is often dismayingly rapid. For this reason we need the constant review of material that we desire to keep fresh in our minds.

Recite the verse or passage you have memorized during the day, before you go to sleep at night, and the first thing in the morning see whether or not it is still with you. Use spare moments of travel on plane or carpool for review. Review pays large dividends in retention and recalling. While you are in the process of learning a new passage, keep repeating the old ones.

Use your scriptures constantly. Closely related to repetition and review is the *use* to which you put what you have learned. One of the fundamental purposes of grouping scriptures about particular subjects is that one might learn those passages that will be usable and most helpful.

Quote scripture every time you get an opportunity, or can make one. Always quote accurately and give the reference. Use scripture portions, in testimony, in prayer, in personal work, in altar work, in talks, in writing—every way you possibly can. As you use these scriptures they will become a part of you, so fixed that neither time nor circumstances can take them from you. If you want the sunset of life to be glorious, make good use of your scriptures when you are young. They will bless you all through life and stand by you when evening shadows gather.

Methods to Assist in Memorization

Verse Memory Cards

The most practical method to aid young people and new Christians in memorizing scripture is the *small card system*. The Topical Memory System of the Navigators uses this practical memorization aid, as do many other plans. In college we learned our Greek alphabet and vocabulary by the card system, and it is a most helpful way to memorize scripture. Build a scripture card packet of your own and it will prove to be a real blessing to you. On one side give the reference and an indication of the topic category in which it falls. On the other side put the scripture verse or passage. Here is an example of a card one might make. The subject and reference are on one side; the actual verse on the other.

```
              II. C. To Point to Holiness
                     1. Provided
                   Hebrews 13:12-13
```

> "Wherefore Jesus also, that he might sanctify the people with his own blood, suffered without the gate.
>
> "Let us go forth therefore unto him without the camp, bearing his reproach."

There are a few suggestions we would make regarding the use of this simple card system.

1. Keep the cards uniform in size.

2. Choose a size most suitable for you. Some may even wish to use the 3" x 5" filing cards. Others will want them smaller. The printed cards such as those suggested earlier in connection with the Memory Plan are usually smaller.

3. Because of the simplicity of this system, do not underestimate its value. Work this plan and your efforts will be crowned with success.

Notice some of the values of this card system for scripture memorization.

1. Its convenience. The cards can be used any time and in any place. These helps may be used going to or from work or school. They can be reviewed on train, plane, car, or bus. It will be most rewarding to review your cards periodically. A few leisure moments can be used to much advantage with this card system. A small number of the cards should be carried at all times in a pocket or purse. Such a practice affords Bible study that would otherwise be forfeited.

2. It is an aid to correct quoting. This simple method of memory training lends itself to correctness. It is so easy to check when we feel we are not in complete mastery of a verse. This means of discipline will give us a grasp of a verse or passage in a minimum amount of time. It is important that we quote accurately the Word of God.

3. It is a boon to remembering the references. In the work of personal evangelism and in public testimony, it is of value to be able to state both the verse or passage and its location. It is of practical value to know where in the Immortal Library the choice treasures are found. Next to the knowledge of something is the ability to locate what you need to know. Knowing the location of a verse or passage helps one to think of that portion in relation to its surroundings and context, and thus a better understanding is gained.

Word Memory Cards

Although a simple method, this plan has been used very effectively. In the case of a short verse, write each word on a separate card. Go over the verse several times with the cards in front of you. Then remove one of the cards and repeat the complete verse. Continue removing cards, not necessarily in sequence, until all the visual aids are gone. By this time the verse should be well fixed in your memory. In the case of longer passages, use phrases or portions of verses on individual cards. This plan can be adapted to your own needs. One might write the verse on a chalkboard or paper and erase a word at a time. Classes or groups can memorize the scriptures by this simple plan.

The Key Word Method

Master the Scripture Memorization Plan first and then keep going. The presentation of these additional methods is to encourage you to continue your work of memorizing the Word. Review the verses of the plan often and then add others and keep at the task of storing the scriptures in your heart and mind. From the individual verses you may now wish to go on to larger passages and to chapters. For this reason we suggest the "Key Word" system of learning. This method can be used by a group or a class where a chalkboard is available.

Here is the procedure:

1. Write the memory work on the chalkboard.
2. Go through each verse and have the young people pick out a key word and underscore it.
3. Go over the entire passage several times, giving special attention to the key words.
4. After repeating a number of times, erase all of the memory work, leaving key words only.
5. Continue repeating the passage or chapter with the aid only of the key words. Keep this up until the portion is mastered.
6. Erase the key words and repeat your passage again.

This method can be used by an individual as well. For example, let us take the 23rd psalm and underscore some key words.

"1. The Lord is my *shepherd;* I shall not want.

"2. He *maketh* me to lie down in green pastures: he *leadeth* me beside the still waters.

"3. He *restoreth* my soul: he *leadeth* me in the paths of righteousness for his name's sake.

"4. Yea, though I walk through the valley of the shadow of death, I will *fear* no evil: for thou art with me; thy rod and they staff they *comfort* me.

"5. Thou *preparest* a table before me in the presence of mine enemies: thou *anointest* my head with oil; my cup runneth over.

"6. Surely goodness and mercy shall *follow* me all the days of my life; and I will *dwell* in the house of the Lord for ever."

Now, write down your list of underscored words and repeat the psalm over and over again, using the key words as guides.

1. shepherd
2. maketh—leadeth
3. restoreth—leadeth
4. fear—comfort
5. preparest—anointest
6. follow—dwell

Then do away with the list of key words and repeat the psalm from memory without any helps. This method should help one to master a chapter in a very short time.

The Challenge Before Us

"This book of the law shall not depart out of thy mouth; but thou shalt meditate therein day and night, that thou mayest observe to do according to all that is written therein: for then thou shalt make thy way prosperous, and then thou shalt have good success" (Josh. 1:8).

* * * *

"The Bible came with our early fathers. And it is not to be doubted that to the free and universal reading of the Bible in that age men were much indebted for their right views of civil liberty. The Bible is a book of doctrine, and a book of morals and a book of religion of special revelation from God; but it is also a book which teaches man his own individual responsibility, his own dignity, his own equality with his fellow men."

—from Daniel Webster's Bunker Hill Address

5

A Scripture Memorization Plan

It is not enough, however, to be acquainted with the theories governing memorization or to know that memorizing the scriptures is a good thing. The time must come to every Christian when he seriously takes hold of the task of systematically committing to memory helpful portions of the Word of God.

It is our earnest hope that you will begin now to build beneath your feet the foundation for an unshakable faith by making portions of the Bible your very own. You cannot afford to neglect this phase of Bible study, for if you hide the Word in your heart it will become a dominant factor in shaping your entire life. The Bible has survived all of its enemies and all of the onslaughts that have been directed toward it through the centuries and it can be just that kind of stable, indestructible force within your life. "The grass withereth, and the flower thereof falleth away: but the word of the Lord endureth for ever" (1 Pet. 1:24-25).

And while you set yourself to this task, it is important to remember that the purpose of memorization is primarily that you might be enriched and helped spiritually. You must think of the Bible as a guide to life. It is not merely a book of recitations. While it is true that certain mechnical methods for more effective memorization are beneficial, and while certain external inducements are profitable in getting you started in learning portions of the Bible, actually these are incidental to the main purpose of memorization. When you are searching for those passages to commit to memory, select those that will assist you the most in your own Christian living. In whatever plan you follow always keep in mind that God has a message for you from His Word. Thus memorization will not become a mechnical process, carried on for superficial rewards or out of a mere sense of duty; nor will it be so many words to be recited on public occasions; rather it will be a hiding in the heart of the very Word of God.

In order that you might be helped in this practical, devotional purpose of scripture memorization, we are presenting here a topical plan with selected verses that relate to all phases of life. It is built upon the premise that every new convert should memorize scriptures in all of the basic areas of Christian living, the idea being that when he is fortified with these scriptures he will be able to combat successfully most of the temptations that come to him.

Immeasurable value is contained in the topical plans of scripture memorization. One of the most complete and effective of these was worked out early in World War II by Dawson Trotman, under the name Navigators. While this was instituted primarily for men in the navy, its outreach has been much broader.

We are indebted to the Navigators' basic idea for the topical plan that follows, which has been developed under the direction of the General Council of the Nazarene Young People's Society.

There are three basic courses composing this plan: the *Beginner's Course,* the *Advanced Course,* and the *Senior Course.* Preceding the *Beginner's Course* are 12 Basic Verses (see Foreword of Part II) which will get you started. After you have memorized these Basic Verses you will move in to complete the *Beginner's Course.* When you have memorized the verses of the *Beginner's Course* you will move to the *Advanced Course.* When you have memorized these verses you will move to the *Senior Course.*

In each of these three courses there are six categories of verses. These are arranged to touch the various phases of Christian life. These verses are vital.

1. To Strengthen Faith
2. To Assure Victory
3. To Point to Holiness
4. To Stimulate Growth
5. To See the Christian's Task
6. To Assist in Soul Winning

Under each of these categories, 6 verses are given. This will mean that each course is composed of 36 verses. In the entire plan there are 108 verses of vital import to every Christian.

When you have finished these verses you will want to continue memorizing other scriptures. Select those you feel will be of greatest value to you. This plan does not intend to limit your memory work. It is intended to assist you in getting started on one of the most thrilling of all experiences.

The scripture verses in the three courses are listed here to make it convenient for you to begin now to memorize them. May God richly bless you as you proceed.

I

BEGINNER'S MEMORY COURSE

A. *To Strengthen Faith*
   1. The Word   *1 Pet. 2:2-3
   2. New Life   2 Cor. 5:17

*These verses marked with the asterisk are the Basic Memory Verses.

    3. Witness   *Rev. 12:11
    4. Assurance   *1 John 5:11
    5. Obedience   *Heb. 5:9
    6. Prayer   *John 16:24

B. *To Assure Victory*

    1. Forgiveness   1 John 1:9
    2. Temptation   *1 Cor. 10:13
    3. Overcome   1 John 5:4
    4. Reward   Jas. 1:12
    5. Holy Spirit   John 14:26
    6. Guidance   Prov. 3:5-6

C. *To Point to Holiness*

    1. Provided   Eph. 1:4
    2. Promised   Joel 2:28-29
    3. Nature of Inbred Sin   Matt. 15:19
    4. Need   Eph. 5:17-18
    5. Conditions   Rom. 12:1-2
    6. The Life   1 Pet. 1:22

D. *To Stimulate Growth*

    1. Love   Gal. 5:22-23
    2. Faith   2 Pet. 1:5-8
    3. Christlikeness   Phil. 1:27
    4. Humility   Jas. 4:10
    5. Fruitfulness   John 15:8
    6. Joy   John 15:11

E. *To See the Christian's Task*

    1. Soul Winning   John 4:35-36
    2. Self-denial   Matt. 6:33
    3. Service   Mark 10:43*b*-44
    4. Strength   Acts 1:8
    5. Warfare   Eph. 6:11
    6. Exalt Christ   1 Cor. 6:20

F. *To Assist in Soul Winning*

    1. Fact of Sin   *Rom. 3:23

    2. Penalty of Sin   *Rom. 6:23
    3. Savior from Sin   *Rom. 5:8
    4. Remedy for Sin   *Eph. 1:7
    5. Repentance of Sin   *Acts 3:19
    6. Believing for Salvation   *John 1:12

II

ADVANCED MEMORY COURSE

A. *To Strengthen Faith*

    1. The Word   Col. 3:16
    2. New Life   1 Cor. 2:12
    3. Witness   1 Pet. 3:15
    4. Assurance   1 John 5:12
    5. Obedience   John 14:21
    6. Prayer   Heb. 4:16

B. *To Assure Victory*

    1. Forgiveness   Acts 2:21
    2. Temptation   2 Cor. 2:14
    3. Overcome   2 Thess. 3:3
    4. Reward   1 Cor. 15:58
    5. Holy Spirit   Rom. 8:26
    6. Guidance   John 16:13

C. *To Point to Holiness*

    1. Provided   Heb. 13:12
    2. Promised   Luke 24:49
    3. Nature of Inbred Sin   Rom. 8:6-7
    4. Need   Rom. 6:6
    5. Conditions   2 Cor. 6:17
    6. The Life   Rom. 6:13

D. *To Stimulate Growth*

    1. Love   Eph. 5:2
    2. Faith   Rom. 10:17
    3. Christlikeness   Eph. 4:32

4. Humility	Rom. 12:3
5. Fruitfulness	John 15:16
6. Joy	1 Pet. 1:8

E. *To See the Christian's Task*

1. Soul Winning	John 9:4
2. Self-denial	Matt. 16:24-25
3. Service	1 John 3:16-18
4. Strength	Matt. 28:19-20
5. Warfare	2 Tim. 2:3-4
6. Exalt Christ	Matt. 10:32-33

F. *To Assist in Soul Winning*

1. Fact of Sin	John 3:19
2. Penalty of Sin	Rom. 5:12
3. Savior from Sin	1 Pet. 3:18
4. Remedy for Sin	1 Pet. 1:18-19
5. Repentance of Sin	Mark 1:14-15
6. Believing for Salvation	1 John 3:23

III

SENIOR MEMORY COURSE

A. *To Strengthen Faith*

1. The Word	Ps. 119:11
2. New Life	Phil. 1:6
3. Witness	1 John 1:3
4. Assurance	John 1:12
5. Obedience	John 15:10
6. Prayer	Phil. 4:6-7

B. *To Assure Victory*

1. Forgiveness	Rom. 10:8-10
2. Temptation	Jude 24-25
3. Overcome	Jas. 4:7
4. Reward	2 Cor. 5:10
5. Holy Spirit	Acts 4:31
6. Guidance	Ps. 37:23

C. *To Point to Holiness*

    1. Provided   Eph. 5:25-27
    2. Promised   1 Thess. 5:23-24
    3. Nature of Inbred Sin   Gal. 5:17
    4. Need   Luke 24:49
    5. Conditions   Rom. 6:6
    6. The Life   1 John 1:7

D. *To Stimulate Growth*

    1. Love   Jude 20-21
    2. Faith   Mark 11:22-24
    3. Christlikeness   1 John 2:6
    4. Humility   Phil. 2:3
    5. Fruitfulness   Gal. 5:22-23
    6. Joy   1 Pet. 4:12-13

E. *To See the Christian's Task*

    1. Soul Winning   Luke 10:2-3
    2. Self-denial   1 Pet. 2:21
    3. Service   Jas. 1:27
    4. Strength   Eph. 6:10
    5. Warfare   Eph. 6:12
    6. Exalt Christ   1 Cor. 1:30-31

F. *To Assist in Soul Winning*

    1. Fact of Sin   Isa. 64:6
    2. Penalty of Sin   Gal. 6:7-8
    3. Savior from Sin   Gal. 3:13
    4. Remedy for Sin   1 Tim. 2:5-6
    5. Repentance of Sin   Acts 16:29-30
    6. Believing for Salvation   Eph. 2:8-9

Think on These Things

John Ruskin said, "All that I have taught of art, everything that I have written, every greatness that has been in any thought of mine, whatever I have done in my life, has simply been due to the fact that when I was a child my mother daily read with me a part of the Bible, and daily made me learn a part of it by heart. That I count confidently the most precious and, upon the whole, the one essential part of all my education."

* * * *

A yard-stick for the cloth, a foot-rule for timber, a sixteen-ounce bit of metal for sugar, truthfulness in speech, honesty in trade, a recognized propriety in cultured circles, a Gray's Anatomy for physicians, a Blackstone for lawyers, and God's Book for strong, winsome life and rest of heart. The famous artist kept the bright colored stones always in sight to tone up his sense of color. The sailor keeps his eye constantly on compass and chart. That's the thing here. Reading it habitually tones up the moral sense, clears the vision, steadies the feet, poises the judgment, stiffens the will, gentles the spirit, comforts the heart, quiets the nerves, and sets the day's work to music.

But, in sharpest contrast with all other books, it makes you face a personal decision. There's no personal appeal in Napoleon or Cromwell. No decision presses in. But here the Man of the Book looks into your face. He calls you to choose. And you do, this way or that. A hand reaches out, and touches your conscience. There's a pullup on your inner motives and your outer conduct.
—S. D. GORDON in *Quiet Talks About Simple Essentials*

* * * *

If you memorize verses on specific Bible doctrines, themes, and principles of Christian living, you will increase your knowledge of God's Word. In addition, you will doubtless be rewarded by having the Holy Spirit prompt you to repeat a verse you have memorized that is the answer to an urgent need in your own life or someone else's.

For your encouragement, studies prove that memory is like a muscle. If it is seldom used, it becomes useless, but if it is constantly exercised, it is strengthened and becomes powerful. Scripture carefully memorized and faithfully reviewed will stay with you the rest of your life.

—CATHERINE BRANDT in *Standard*

* * * *

Some time ago I came across the story of a small boy who carried a Bible to his grandmother with the inquiry as to whose Book it was. When Grandma had informed him that this was "God's Book," he responded, "Then don't you think we ought to give it back to Him? Nobody here seems to be using it!"

Someone has said, "Reading the Bible is good, studying it is better, but memorizing it is best of all."

* * * *

THE SECRET OF BIBLE STUDY

1. Study it through. Never begin a day without mastering a verse.

2. Pray it in. Never leave your Bible until the passage you have studied is a part of your very being.

3. Put it down. The thought God gives you, put it in the margin of your Bible or notebook.

4. Work it out. Live the truth you get through all the hours of the day.

5. Pass it on. Seek to tell somebody what you have learned.

—J. WILBUR CHAPMAN

God's Unchanging Word

For feelings come and feelings go,
  And feelings are deceiving.
My warrant is the Word of God;
  Naught else is worth believing.

Though all my heart should feel condemned
  For want of some sweet token,
There is One greater than my heart
  Whose Word cannot be broken.

I'll trust in God's unchanging Word
  Till soul and body sever;
For, though all things shall pass away,
  His Word shall stand forever.

—Martin Luther

6

Additional Suggestions for Memorization

The story is told of a town in England that had its beginning around a well, the water of which contained curative properties. People drinking the water found restored health. In the course of time an inn was built near the well, then a blacksmith's shop, a store, and some homes, until the village grew into an organized community. But years later, when a traveler asked the village clerk for the location of the well, the clerk shook his head in embarrassment and said, "This is the unfortunate part, we have forgotten the location of the well."

How true a picture this is of much of our country's life today! Our fathers came here to find political freedom, religious freedom, and all the freedoms that go with them. To this end they erected their churches, opened their schools, wrote their laws, and established their homes around the Word of God and the family altar. Before he was president, Woodrow Wilson had become America's most trustworthy historian, and he wrote: "America was born to exemplify that devotion to the elements of righteousness which are derived from the revelation of Holy Scripture."

Yet today many a successful American who still bears in his life the imprint of the Church and the afterglow of the Christian home has in the midst of his material success forgotten God, ignored the Church, neglected to pray, and ceased to read the Bible. If asked the source of his stimulus and his inspiration, he too would have to admit that he has forgotten the location of the well from which has come the life-giving water of freedom.[1]

The purpose of this manual is to help the Christian young person and new convert to keep close to that fountain of life. Many a person has regretted later that early in life he did not form the habit of memorizing systematically the Word of God. This chapter presents some additional suggestions for Bible memorization.

Passages to Memorize

Verses with Personal Significance

The writer hurried to the hospital room and to the bedside of one yet young but taken with a serious illness from which many never recover. It was a long, hard pull back to health and strength. One of the greatest boons during that struggle was a verse of scripture and here it is: "Fear thou not; for I am with thee: be not dismayed; for I am thy God: I will strengthen thee; yea, I will help thee; yea, I will uphold thee with the right hand of my righteousness" (Isa. 41:10). That verse was too important to this person ever to be forgotten.

The Bible speaks to the human heart and meets our needs. Without a doubt there is a verse or passage that has been of special help and blessing to you. Commit those words to memory and never let them go.

Significant Verses

The particular verses or passages that have helped you in a special way ought to be stored in your mind and heart. We would do well to give attention to the passages that have been the favorites of Christians down through the centuries, for these scriptures have wealth immeasurable. For instance, there are the promises of God. The precious promises of the Bible number into the thousands and here is a fruitful field for soul enrichment. "Whereby are given unto us exceeding great and precious promises: that by these ye might be partakers of the divine nature" (2 Pet. 1:4). For an entire year in a recent pastorate we adopted the plan of a "Promise-of-the-week." Some have called them "Handles of Power." They proved to be a source of spiritual blessing to the people in their endeavors to live for God. We suggest that, as one of many plans, you commit these and others of the promises to memory. Here is a list to get you started:

1. Ps. 37:4
2. Ps. 121:7-8
3. Rev. 2:10
4. Rev. 3:21
5. Isa. 41:10
6. Matt. 6:33
7. Luke 12:32
8. Ps. 84:11
9. 1 Pet. 5:4
10. Isa. 65:24
11. Phil. 4:19
12. 2 Chron. 7:14
13. Joel 2:21
14. John 14:13
15. 1 Cor. 10:13
16. Rom. 8:28
17. 2 Pet. 5:6-7
18. Rev. 22:14
19. Mark 9:23
20. Ps. 27:5
21. Isa. 40:31
22. Matt. 5:6
23. Ps. 37:5
24. Isa. 43:2
25. Ps. 91:1
26. Ps. 55:22
27. Isa. 40:29
28. Matt. 19:29
29. Jas. 1:12
30. John 12:26
31. Ps. 125:2
32. Heb. 11:16
33. Isa. 42:16
34. Heb. 9:28
35. Mark 11:24
36. 1 Pet. 1:3-4
37. Phil. 4:7
38. Luke 18:29-30
39. Deut. 33:27*a*
40. John 16:33
41. John 11:25-26*a*
42. 2 Cor. 12:9
43. Isa. 57:15
44. Heb. 7:25
45. Ps. 34:7
46. 2 Cor. 6:17-18
47. John 14:27
48. Rev. 21:7
49. Isa. 35:10
50. 2 Pet. 3:9
51. Rev. 3:12
52. Matt. 1:21

The Highly Significant Passages

There are also the significant passages that have been profitable to the children of God down through the years. There are those paragraphs and portions of the Word that have lifted to serene heights the souls of the saints throughout the many centuries. They will be very porfitable to you. Let me suggest a few:

1. The Master's Blesseds—Matt. 5:1-16
2. The Fruit of the Spirit—Gal. 5:22-26
3. The Christian Graces—2 Pet. 1:5-9
4. The Importance of God in Youth—Eccles. 12:1-7
5. Here's Strength for You—Isa. 40:28-31
6. Paul's Great Prayer—Eph. 3:14-21
7. The Lord's Prayer—Matt. 6:9*b*-13
8. When God Is Supreme—Matt. 6:24-34
9. The Mind of Christ—Phil. 2:5-11
10. The Love of God—Rom. 8:31-39
11. Christ as Our Example—Heb. 12:1-6
12. The High Privilege of Sonship—1 John 3:1-3

The "Golden Chapters"

Commit to memory also some of the "Golden Chapters" of the Bible. One list I have seen gives 140 "Golden Chapters." Let me indicate, however, a few that would be an abundant source of soul nourishment:

1. Paul's Hymn of Love—1 Corinthians 13
2. The Hymn of an Old Shepherd—Psalm 23
3. The Suffering Servant—Isaiah 53
4. Christ's Message on Security—John 14
5. A Practical Guide for Life—Romans 12
6. The Song of the Traveler—Psalm 121
7. The Ways of Life—Psalm 1

8. A Song for the Sanctuary—Psalm 84
9. The Gospel in the Old Testament—Isaiah 55
10. Faith at Its Best—Psalm 91
11. The Song of the King Triumphant—Psalm 24
12. The Final Invitation—Revelation 22
13. The Hymn of Holy Confidence—Psalm 46
14. The Way of Holiness—Isaiah 35
15. The Doxology—Psalm 100

Everybody Loves a Story

The Bible is a storehouse of literary treasure. Both the Old and New Testaments are filled with unusual stories. Difference of opinion would make it difficult to list the 25 greatest stories of the Bible. We list here a few of the New Testament stories that might well be committed to memory:

1. The Prodigal Son—Luke 15:11-32
2. The Lame Man of Bethesda—John 5:1-9
3. The Good Samaritan—Luke 10:25-37
4. The Story of Forgiveness—Matt. 18:21-35
5. The Shipwreck of Paul—Acts 27
6. The Marriage Feast—Matt. 22:1-14
7. The Ten Virgins—Matt. 25:1-13
8. The Lad by the Lake—John 6:1-14
9. The Calming of the Tempest—Matt. 8:23-27
10. The Rich Man and Lazarus—Luke 16:19-31

Verses to Assist in Soul Winning

Winning others for Christ was everybody's job in the early Christian Church. Today we so often expect the pastor, evangelist, teacher, missionary, or specialized Christian worker to do all the witnessing and soul winning. A desire to win others is a normal part of the life that is truly Christian and entirely surrendered to Jesus Christ. Upon every Christian is thrust the responsibility of the Great Commission. "Go ye therefore, and teach [make disciples or Christians of] all nations . . ." (Matt. 28:19). We need to store the scriptures in our minds so that we will have them in a time when we have opportunity to lead someone to Jesus Christ. Whatever you do, never parade your ability to quote scripture. The Word must become such a part of us that we will be able to quote applicable verses to the one with whom we are dealing and do it with adeptness but without show or strain.

Memorize those verses that will enable you to help someone to a saving knowledge of Jesus Christ. Mark those passages that will be of special use to you in helping others to find Christ and salvation. Those you try to help will almost invariably have excuses. Be prepared with the Word to meet these objections. Here are several suggestions to help you in soul winning in addition to those already given.

(a) For those who do not see their need of a Savior

1. Isa. 53:6
2. Isa. 55:6-7
3. Jer. 17:9
4. Matt. 7:21
5. John 3:3, 7
6. John 3:18
7. John 3:36
8. 1 Cor. 6:9*a*
9. Titus 3:5
10. Heb. 2:3
11. Heb. 9:27
12. Jas. 2:10
13. Jas. 4:17
14. 1 Pet. 4:18
15. 1 John 1:8
16. 1 John 3:8
17. Rev. 20:15
18. Rev. 22:12

(b) For those who prefer a later time

1. Isa. 55:6-7
2. Josh. 24:15
3. 1 Kings 18:21
4. Prov. 27:1
5. Matt. 24:44
6. Luke 12:19-20
7. Acts 22:16
8. 2 Cor. 6:2

(c) For those who need instruction in holiness

1. John 17:17, 19
2. Acts 1:4-5
3. Acts 2:39
4. Acts 26:16-18
5. Matt. 5:48
6. 1 Thess. 4:3*a*
7. 1 Thess. 4:7
8. Heb. 6:1
9. Heb. 12:14
10. 1 Pet. 1:15-16
11. Gal. 2:20

THE USE OF THE BIBLE FOR ORAL READINGS

The use of the Bible in the field of vocal expression is much neglected. Such use has been called "the wonderful, almost-unexplored territory of the Word of God." There are many types of interpretative readings, recitations, and oral expressions both in religious and secular fields. Not enough use, however, has been made of the Bible as a source for oral readings. We would do well if we would give the Word of God our consideration for this purpose.

The reward for work in this area is twofold. There is the value gained by the reader who commits to memory the passages suitable for this purpose. There is also the value to those who hear the oral readings. Here is a ministry indeed, for when the Bible is given effective vocal expression much good is accomplished. Pliny the Younger wrote: "We are much more affected by words which we hear, for though what we read in books may be more pointed, yet there is something in the voice, the look, the carriage, and the gesture of the speaker that makes a deeper impression on the mind." The value of interpretative and oral readings is above question. If this were not true, one may as well give the material to an audience and let them read it.

Some Starting Suggestions

1. *Have a thorough understanding of the passage.* It is indispensable that the message be grasped before it can be

properly given. Since words are symbols, you must endeavor to find out what the author really means. Words you do not understand should be looked up in the dictionary. If there are characters in the passages, take a Bible dictionary and learn something about those people. The more clearly you understand the portion, the better will your interpretation be.

2. *Give time to meditation.* There is no place here for superficial effort. No matter how many times one may go over the material, it will not become a part of you until you have spent some time in quiet meditation upon it. You must absorb the spirit and the mood of the selection if you would pass them on to your hearers. Proper time spent in meditation will help one to keep away from the false and the superficial. The task of the oral reader is to stir up in others the meaning of the writer. It is possible to pronounce each word clearly and correctly and yet fail to interpret the meaning of the passage to the listener.

3. *Use your imagination.* The people must become real to you and the ideas and situations must be vivid and powerful in your own thinking and feeling. Don't expect others to see something that you do not really see. You will have to walk along with Naaman, the Syrian general and leper, to the banks of muddy Jordan if you expect to compel others to see a man cleansed from leprosy.

4. *Aim to read expressively, not mechanically.* One should have proper enunciation and every syllable should be crystal-clear, but one dare not be so conscious of technique that the reading is done in a mechanical way. Endeavor always to be natural. I heard the famous evangelist, Gypsy Smith, say that if he had the privilege of playing only one note on the piano it would be "B natural."

5. *Give attention to the fundamentals of expression.* The use of the Bible for oral readings will demand the best you have to give to it. If one would become effective and efficient,

there must be concern for the fundamentals of expression, such as modulation, rhythm, change of ideas and pitch, inflection, emotion, enunciation, imagination, movement, proper pace, and the change of pace.

6. *Preparation is indispensable.* The learning process is gradual and the preparation anything but hasty. It takes time and hard work to make proper preparation, but success comes only that way. It is either prepare or fail.

7. *Give consideration to ideas and not merely to words.* We need to get the main idea of a passage first and then relate the other ideas to this central truth. Every part of a passage must be related to the whole. This is basic for understanding and for expression. Dr. S. S. Curry says in *Lessons in Expression:* "All memory should be of ideas. The thought should be reproduced, idea should follow idea by a natural and logical sequence. . . . A mechnical use of memory will make all expression artificial. . . . The mind is simply recalling words, and does not re-create ideas; such practice encourages the student to speak without thought, causes his voice to become cold, his memory to become superficial, and his relation to literature to become one of indifference."[2]

8. *Look for the contrast and comparison of ideas.* For example, notice the evident contrast in these words of Jesus as recorded in Matt. 7:24-27.

"Therefore whosoever heareth these sayings of mine, and doeth them, I will liken unto a wise man, which built his house upon a rock: and the rain descended, and the floods came, and the winds blew, and beat upon that house; and it fell not: for it was founded upon a rock."
(Note: heareth, doeth, rock.)

"And every one that heareth these sayings of mine, and doeth them not, shall be likened unto a foolish man, which built his house upon the sand: and the rain descended, and the floods came, and the winds blew, and beat upon that

house; and it fell: and great was the fall of it."
(Note: heareth, doeth not, sand.)

In the story of the Good Samaritan, Luke 10:25-37, we have another example of contrast and comparison. Here we have four classifications of men:

> The Hurt Man—robbed and wounded by the wayside
> The Hurting Man—the robber
> The Heedless Man—the priest and the Levite
> The Helping Man—the Good Samaritan
> (Author of outline unknown)

The central figure in the story is, of course, the Good Samaritan. The other figures are related clearly to the central character. One ought to look always for the central idea and then the related truths.

Selections for Oral Bible Readings
(Supplied by Audrey J. Williamson)

A. *Narratives with Swift-moving Action*

A word of introduction or setting, before reading, is often helpful.

1. 2 Kings 5—Naaman the Leper
2. Luke 10:25-37—The Good Samaritan
3. Gen. 22:1-14—Abraham's Test of Faith
4. Luke 15:11-32—The Parable of the Father
5. Luke 7:36-50—Jesus in the House of Simon
6. Dan. 5:1-30—Belshazzar's Feast
7. 1 Kings 18:17-40—Elijah's Contest on Carmel
8. John 4:4-30—At Sychar's Well
9. John 9:1-38—Healing of the Blind Man

B. *Passages That Teach, Inspire, or Comfort*
   1. James 3—The Tongue
   2. Matt. 5:3-16—The State of the Blessed
   3. Matt. 6:19-34—Seeking the Kingdom
   4. Matt. 7:7-27—Doers of the Word
   5. John 10:1-18—The Good Shepherd
   6. Psalm 19—The Revelation of God
   7. 1 Corinthians 13—Perfect Love
   8. John 14:1-18—The Comforter
   9. Revelation 22—The Holy City

C. *Personal and Lyric Expressions of Praise and Thanksgiving*
   1. Psalm 27—Faith in the Power of God
   2. Psalm 8—The Excellency of Our God
   3. Psalm 34—A Testimony of Praise
   4. Psalm 19—The Christian's Resting Place
   5. Psalm 100—A Psalm of Praise

D. *Exalted and Epic Passages of Oratoric Character*
   1. Acts 26:2-29—Paul's Defense Before Agrippa
   2. Isaiah 35—The Way of Holiness
   3. Isaiah 55—The Power of the Word
   4. Isaiah 53—The Suffering Savior
   5. Isaiah 40—The Incomparable God
   6. Psalm 24—The Advent of the King

Audrey J. Williamson, who provided for us the "Selections for Oral Readings," writes: "If even *one* person ventures out into the wonderful, almost-unexplored territory of the Word of God in the field of vocal expression, as a result of this effort I shall be repaid."

A Final Tribute to the Word

Book of Books

Thou art a lamp whose flickering light is old;
  Yet, in the darkened hours of earth's new day,
  It shines anew, to mark the certain way
Of joy and peace and glories still untold.

Thou art a flame which purifies the gold
  Of man's true self, and burns the dross away.
  Misshapen by the forms of baser clay,
Tomorrow's life must find thy nobler mold.

Thou art a blazing sun whose warming light
  Still dries the dew of penitential tears,
Gives life to all the world, makes clear to sight
  The power of truth, the love that conquers fears,
O Book of books, our lamp, our flame, our sun,
Reveal! Refine! Inspire! till heaven is won.[3]

—Alfred Grant Walton

A Closing Prayer

O Lord, I am Thine and the Bible is my Book. Help me to ever give Thy Word its rightful place in my daily life. May I make it truly mine by taking a portion of the time Thou hast given me, to read, to study, and to memorize the Word. By this revelation let me live and let me die. O Lord, "I will delight myself in thy statutes: I will not forget thy word." Amen.

The Bible Is Your Book

1. Read it regularly.
2. Study it carefully.
3. Carry it consistently.
4. Memorize it systematically.

Notes

Part I

CHAPTER 1
MAKE THE BIBLE YOURS

1. From a clipping, source unknown.

2. George F. Pentecost, *"In the Volume of the Book"* (New York and Chicago: A. S. Barnes & Co., 1885), pp. 56-75.

3. Arthur T. Pierson, *The Bible and Spiritual Life* (New York: Fleming H. Revell Co.), pp. 49-50.

4. Mildred Cable and Francesca French, *The Spark and the Flame* (London: Annual Report of the British and Foreign Bible Society, 1948), p. 49.

CHAPTER 2
PRACTICAL GUIDES FOR BIBLE READING

1. Walter Scott.

2. John Wesley, in the *King's Business.*

CHAPTER 3
SIMPLE METHODS FOR BIBLE STUDY

1. Wilbur M. Smith, *Profitable Bible Study* (Boston: W. A. Wilde Company, 1939), p. 33.

2. WHO WERE THEY? (1) Abraham, (2) Joseph, (3) Deborah, (4) Elijah, (5) Haggai, (6) Jacob, (7) Daniel, (8) Elisha and the students who watched and laughed, (9) Esther, (10) Moses, (11) Malachi

3. Kansas City: Beacon Hill Press of Kansas City.

4. Ibid.

5. Pentecost, *"In the Volume of the Book,"* pp. 49-50.

6. William T. Ellis, *"Billy Sunday," The Man and His Message* (Philadelphia: The John C. Winston Company, 1914), pp. 259-60.

Part II

CHAPTER 6

ADDITIONAL SUGGESTIONS FOR MEMORIZATION

1. *The Bible—Book of Freedom,* The Board of Manager's Report for 1950 (American Bible Society, 450 Park Ave., New York 22, N.Y.), pp. 3-4.

2. S. S. Curry, *Lessons in Expression* (Boston: The Expression Company, 1895), pp. 274-75.

3. Taken from *The Fountain of Life,* a brochure prepared for the observance of Universal Bible Sunday, 1937, by the American Bible Society.

Bibliography

American Bible Society, 450 Park Avenue, New York 22, N.Y., leaflets and pamphlets.

Cable, Mildred; and French, Francesca. *The Spark and the Flame.* London: The British and Foreign Bible Society, 1948.

Cook, Robert A. *Now That I Believe.* Chicago: The Moody Press, 1949.

Gray, James M. *How to Master the English Bible.* Chicago: The Moody Press, 1951.

Oxford University Press, American Branch, New York, N.Y. *The Bible Reader's Companion,* 1925.

Pentecost, George F. *"In the Volume of the Book."* New York and Chicago: A. S. Barnes & Company, 1885.

Pierson, A. T. *Keys to the Word.* New York: Charles C. Cook.

―――. *The Bible and Spiritual Life.* New York: Fleming H. Revell Company.

Riley, John E. *The Golden Stairs.* Kansas City: Beacon Hill Press, 1947.

Smith, Wilbur M. *Profitable Bible Study.* Boston: W. A. Wilde Company, 1939.

Thomas, W. H. Griffith. *And God Spake These Words.* Chicago: The Bible Institute Colportage Association, 1926.

―――. *Methods of Bible Study.* Chicago: The Bible Institute Colportage Association, 1926.